DATING VIOLENCE

DATING VIOLENCE

TRUE STORIES OF HURT AND HOPE

JOHN HICKS

The Millbrook Press
Brookfield, Connecticut

Library of Congress Cataloging-in-Publication Data
Hicks, John, 1951–
Dating violence : true stories of hurt and hope / John Hicks.
p.   cm.
Includes bibliographical references and index.
Summary: Interviews with abusers and victims form the basis of this
discussion of the characteristics and dangers of unhealthy relationships,
the importance of honest communication, and cooperative ways of
resolving conflict.
ISBN 1-56294-654-4 (Lib. bdg.)
1. Dating violence—United States—Juvenile literature. 2. Teenagers—
Abuse of—United States—Juvenile literture. 3. Interpersonal relations—
United States—Juvenile literature. [1. Dating violence. 2. Interpersonal
relations.] I. Title.
HQ801.83h53   1996
362.88—dc20   95-52265   CIP   AC

Published by The Millbrook Press, Inc.
2 Old New Milford Road
Brookfield, Connecticut 06804

CONTENTS

MICHELLE'S STORY

My dad's in the Air Force, and we moved to Germany when I was eight. We returned when I was twelve, almost thirteen, and Will lived right next to me when we moved on base. He was almost three years older, so he kinda took me under his wing. We spent a lot of time together, and we developed a very strong friendship. He was very protective, very mature. He had a lot of status among our group of friends. Everybody looked up to Will. Everybody respected him a lot.

After a few months I started developing feelings for him. But I made it very clear that this was new to me, that I wasn't ready to have sex. He scared me with all of his sexual experience. I was like, "I don't want to do that yet." He said he was fine with that. He'd say, "I don't want to lose you as a friend, so I'd much rather wait."

Will started smoking pot now and then, and he started to do weird things, like hitting on my best friend. He also started running away. One night Will's dad, who was alcoholic, came looking for him with a shotgun. Things got so chaotic that the base authorities stepped in and forced Will's father to go into treatment. His mother was the complete opposite, she thought Will could do no wrong. There was still a lot of fighting back and forth, so she sent Will to live with his uncle thinking maybe that he would calm down.

I'd see him when he came down to visit. We talked about having sex then, and I decided that I was ready. The only problem was that he was interested in my best friend, too. So I told Will, "It's your decision." He called from his uncle's to ask me to be his girlfriend. I asked him what made him decide to go out with me, and he said, "I already asked Suzanne, and she said no." At the time I didn't mind being his second choice, because I would be with him, and that's all that mattered.

It was supposed to be a surprise that he was moving back in a couple of weeks, but I found out and I was very excited. When the day finally came, my family was having a yard sale, so I had to stay home. He came by, and then went to see some other friends. I found out later that he had gone to Suzanne's house and made a pass at her. When I confronted him, we got in a big argument over it. He said that she had made the pass at him. I really don't know what happened. I just know that somebody made a pass at somebody, or it was a mutual thing, and we proceeded to break up. At that time everybody was on my side. Even his best friend Shep thought he was a jerk because he dumped me.

About two weeks later I was in my room about eleven o'clock, and someone threw rocks at my window. I was very surprised to see Will standing outside. I said, "You swore that you were never gonna speak to me again." He proceeded to tell me he was miserable with Suzanne, that he couldn't live without me, just everything I wanted to hear. So we got back together. I couldn't tell my parents, because of what he did to me the first time. They knew that we were friends again, but they didn't know that we were going out.

When we started dating, Will kept bringing up the topic of sex. He was very persuasive. He'd say, "You're just afraid because you've never done it before," or, "I just want to show you what it's all about." I was like, "No! I don't want to look back and say I lost my virginity at thirteen." He didn't get angry, he just kept up the pressure. He tried to get me to do other things, some stuff I felt okay about. I didn't have a problem with making out.

One time we were with Shep and his girlfriend, and Will wanted to perform oral sex on me. I said, "No, I don't want to do this, especially in your best friend's room." He got very upset and just took off. We all got worried, so we went out looking for him. We gave up and walked back to Shep's house, and Will was waiting there. I apologized a gazillion times, but he wouldn't talk about what happened. He just said he wanted to go home.

We were walking the back way to my house on base. We were cutting up and teasing, like nothing was wrong. Suddenly he threw his hands up in the air and walked away. It was ten-thirty at night, and I was scared out of my mind. I don't care that it's an army base, it's still not safe. I walked home very carefully. To this day, I will not walk in the dark by myself.

The next day we made up, and he said, "You just did this to piss me off, to put me down in front of my friends." And I accepted that it was all my fault. He was very good at getting me to doubt what I saw and felt—very persuasive. I promised I wouldn't do anything to make him mad anymore.

Will's mom had started sending him to a shrink, which was not doing any good. He'd leave, be gone for two or three days, and his mother just couldn't stand it. She wanted to put him into a Center for in-patient counseling. He'd have screaming fights with her on the phone, with him crying and yelling, "Don't do this to me." I was right there, consoling him through all this. He said, "Don't you leave me, 'cause I can't live without you." She popped him into the Center two weeks before my fourteenth birthday. . . . I was hurt that he would be missing that. I became totally and completely lost.

A few weeks later I went down there to see him. He had this unreal look on his face when he saw me. He was just floored. He said, "What are you doing here? I'm so glad you're here." The rule at the Center was you couldn't have any physical touch while visiting. He said, "We can find ways around this," then pulled me in this conference room and enveloped me in a huge hug. When he kissed me he was all over me. He seemed different, more aggressive than I had seen him before. But I took it as a sign he missed me. The whole time we were in there he kept touching me, saying stuff like, "This is what I want to do when we get home. I can't wait to be with you." I just shrugged it off. I figured he had just been locked away too long, so it didn't bother me.

I had started high school the beginning of September, a big change for me. Will was released the end of September, and the first day he was out, we were in his room, kinda making out, kinda talking. All of a sudden he got up and started changing clothes. He said, "I hear so-and-so's been talking trash about me, I have to go and teach him a lesson." We had several tense situations that week. It was just one thing after another, everything was setting him off.

About a week after he had been released, we were upstairs in his room, making out pretty heavily, and someone came to the door. He got up and I said, "Where are you goin'?" He told me he had business to take care of and I couldn't come. So he left, and I waited, and I waited, and I waited. Finally I said, "Forget this," and I went out looking for him. I walked around, and I just poked my head around the corner, and there he was with Shep and another guy. They were all very quiet, very serious. Will saw me and he walked toward me and said, "I thought I told you to stay upstairs." I told him I got tired of waiting, and he said, "I'll be there when I get there, don't leave."

So I went back up to his room, and about ten minutes later he opened his door, and I was sitting on the bed. He said, "You have some explaining to do." He was very firm, his eyes were very cold. He proceeded to tell me I had been sleeping with another guy while he was away at the Center. I said no, but he kept saying, "That's not what I heard."

He kept saying that. I don't know if that was just to get him more angry, to say those words over and over again. Finally, I just said, "I'm not going to sit here and argue about this. You obviously believe someone other than me. I am your girlfriend, and I have been for several months now, but I'm not going to sit here and take this from you. When you calm down we'll talk."

As I got up to leave, he pushed me down. He was easily twice my size at that time. He proceeded to call me all sorts of names, some of them I can remember, some of them I can't. They were very graphic, very derogatory. At that point I was scared. He looked at me and he said, "You bitch, I'm going to teach you a lesson. You're gonna show me what you did." He grabbed my legs and pulled me down. He held me down with his legs on mine, and grabbed my arms. I couldn't move. And he raped me. The first time.

I couldn't go to my parents because they had forbid me to see him. When we got back together, he turned me against my best friend Suzanne in a big way. I thought there was no one I could tell. Where could I go? Everywhere I went, he was right there with me, and I lived right next door. If I wasn't even safe in my home, then I might as well be with him. That's exactly what I thought.

The abuse continued for a month and a half, including verbal abuse, lots of sexual abuse. There were days when he was wonderful, you couldn't have asked for better. And there were days when he wasn't. He was very manipulative and he knew how to get inside my head and play with my mind. I know that every time he wanted to have sex, or whatever, I relented in the end. I put up with it because he was my boyfriend. I thought, "Well, I love him, maybe this is what it's all about." But he had me afraid, too.

People don't realize that abuse can come in many different forms. He didn't have to touch me to abuse me. There was a lot of intimidation. He would threaten me time and time again. "If you don't do this. . ." or "If you don't shut up, I'm going to put your head through that wall." I'd seen the holes that he'd put with his fist. I didn't want to attempt it with my head.

I was forced to perform oral sex on several occasions. It happened a couple of times in my house, mostly in his. Several times his mom was right downstairs. He was never loud. When we were fighting we were loud. . .but when he did that he was very calm, his voice very even.

We were fighting a lot of the time. If someone pissed him off, I usually heard about it, or was the recipient of the anger. I remember one time I thought nobody else was home. We had gone to his house after school and gotten into an argument. He just shouted all sorts of names at me. When I came downstairs, Shep was sitting on the couch.

I asked him, "How long have you been here?" And he said, "Oh, about thirty minutes." Will came back down and he wouldn't even talk to me, so I left. Shep had to have known what was going on up there. He had to. He knew and never said anything to me, never said anything to Will. But we were all pretty scared of Will.

He broke up with me before the abuse stopped. He just looked at me one day and said, "I've had enough of you. I don't love you anymore." I was crushed, totally devastated. I just felt so used.

A couple of days afterwards, I'd gone over to his house to talk to him and see if we could make amends. No amends for me. He forced me to have sex and I just laid there and went numb. I blocked it out, like I wasn't even there.

He verbally assaulted me at school one day: screaming, yelling, threatening, all of it. That time I went right to our vice-principal, who took care of that situation. I guess because it had happened in public, I was able to tell my mom about it, and she went over to talk to his mom. She came back and told me, "You just have to keep your distance." So even after breaking up, it was still my fault. If he got upset, I still took the blame.

I don't remember a lot of the school year after that. I was miserable. I kept believing that I'd lost the one person for me. And my friends didn't help. They kept telling me, "He's miserable without you." You'd never know it—he wouldn't even speak to me. I attempted suicide once about two weeks afterwards. Then one of my friends expressed an interest in him, so he began having sex with her and left me alone. We moved off base a few months later. Not long after that, I tried suicide again.

It wasn't until about two years later that I realized Will had raped me. In November of my junior year, I began having flashbacks. I'll never forget the first time, I was sitting in the middle of church. Boom—there he was. It's like I could see, hear, and feel him right there in front of me. The nightmares started very shortly after that.

I didn't tell anybody. My moods were up and down. I was very hysterical a lot of the time. Finally, I called my friend who lives out of state and I told her what was happening. I said, "I'm afraid to tell anyone else, because I don't want anything to happen to him." She goes, "Stop right there. If you tell, you're not doing anything because he crossed the boundaries, not you." She said, "You're not to blame for this, it was not your fault." And it was shocking to me that I was still taking the blame for what he had done. It was then that I was able to break the silence and get some help.

INTRODUCTION

Violence is fast becoming the most important issue our society is facing. Television news, newspapers, and magazine stories recount assaults, robberies, and murders in unprecedented numbers. The increase in gun violence especially has brought tragedy out of crowded inner cities into the areas of life that were once thought sacred: our homes, schools, social clubs, playgrounds, commuter trains. Although the incidence of some types of crimes is actually decreasing, our public perception of violence is intensifying. And the number of violent crimes against individuals is increasing.

The common belief is that violent acts are committed by professional criminals, strangers who randomly invade our safe and comfortable lives, commit a crime against an unsuspecting person, and then disappear, taking a brief spin through the overworked criminal justice system or having a short stay in an overcrowded jail before being released to offend again. This is an accurate picture of one segment of those who commit violent crimes. These criminals are people whose lives have deteriorated for a number of reasons, who are unable to act with a sense of morality or to function within the rules of society. Their tragic and often senseless crimes are only the most publicized offenses, not the most common.

The violence that affects the majority of us occurs much closer to home. Almost 40 percent of violent crimes are committed by people that we know, people that we live with, or people that we love. According to Department of Justice statistics, homicide and simple assault are the least likely crimes to be committed by a stranger. The National Crime Survey estimates that about 10 percent of these nonstranger or "domestic" assaults are committed against women by boyfriends or ex-boyfriends. More than 3 percent of all murders in the United States are the result of someone's being killed by a girlfriend or boyfriend.

These estimates may be low. Victims report crimes more often if they are committed by strangers than by the victim's friends or relatives. By any estimate, violence in intimate relationships is a major issue facing all of us. Former surgeon general C. Everett Koop has called this "an overwhelming moral, economic and public health burden that our society can no longer bear."

As overwhelming as this problem is, it remains hidden. Domestic assaults usually happen in private, and the people who are affected often strive to keep it a secret. The shame involved in either being battered by or hurting someone we care for makes it hard to tell anyone, even those closest to us. People in abusive relationships often work hard at making it seem as if nothing is wrong. They try to convince themselves and others that "it's not really that bad," or that "it doesn't happen all the time."

Certain attitudes in our culture about the roles of men and women sometimes make it seem natural for one person in a relationship to make the decisions for both. It is hard to see when these types of relationships become "institutionalized" forms of abuse, partly because they're around us all the time. It is common for one partner to take a more dominant role (this often happens even in couples of the same sex). When the other person decides to confront the inequality of power, however, there is often a struggle for control. Sometimes that struggle escalates to include the use of force—that's when someone gets hurt.

Although force doesn't always result in physical injury, it always results in harm. At the very least, it breaks down trust, damages the self-esteem of the injured partner, and creates the fear that it will happen again.

Many myths about dating violence are commonly held beliefs among teenagers. Many think that it is a sign of love or that violence can improve a dating relationship. Some believe that it will stop when the couple gets married or lives together. Another often fatal misconception is that the need for one partner to control the other will automatically stop after the couple breaks up. Separating is an important step in dealing with an abusive relationship, but to ensure that the violence doesn't continue, the victim must get outside support and protection to break the silence and ask for help.

In this book, young people who have been hurt by—or have hurt—someone they love tell their stories in their own words. None of these kids fits the description of a criminal—they knew their victims and their actions were not random. They represent a group of young people from every type of background, rich and poor, who live in a variety of places, from housing projects to farms. Their names and some details have been changed to protect their confidentiality, but the stories these kids tell are real. These young people will tell us about their experiences when starting to date, the kind of person they're looking for, and what they think someone is looking for in them. As their relationships with their partners become more serious, we'll hear about what goes wrong and their attempts to make things right. We'll also hear stories of hope, how change is possible, and how they start over.

This is not a self-help book. Dating violence is not something you tackle on your own. A book can give you information and prompt you to think, but it can't provide safety and support—those are things you have to ask for. But reading this book will help answer a number of questions:

- What mistakes do people make early on in dating?
- How can I make dating safer for me? For my friends?
- What do I do if a friend is battering someone or being battered?
- How do I know if I am in a battering relationship?
- What do I do if I think I am?
- Whom do I tell, and where can I go for help?

This book is for young people who are already dating or who are about to start dating. It tells the truth about dating violence in order to prevent it from happening, but it is also a guidebook to enable young people to build trusting, open relationships based on equality and mutual consent.

CHAPTER ONE
LOOKING FOR THE RIGHT RELATIONSHIP

> There were things I thought a guy was sup-
> posed to do in a relationship. I was looking for
> somebody like that, somebody who would just
> treat me good, and to have fun with. I've been
> looking for a lifelong mate since I was twelve,
> maybe. Maybe before then, I don't know.
>
> — Linda

This is a book about dating, about young people coming together to build relationships. It is about what can
go wrong—the pain and isolation of abuse; how to stop
the hurt and hurting; where to go for support and safety.
But this book is also about what can go right—what
makes a good relationship; how to avoid setting up
yourself or your partner to fail; how to approach conflict in ways that make a relationship and the two people
in it safer and stronger.

DREAMS, HOPES, AND WISHES

Since before we could talk, each of us has received
thousands, maybe millions of messages about members
of our own sex and the opposite sex and about how

and why people are attracted to each other. We probably began sorting out these messages at about the age of five. Many adolescents' ideas about love have a "storybook romance" quality, because, like Linda, most people have been carrying those messages around since childhood.

> When we first got together, it was like some sort of fairytale. I was the "School Princess" and he was the "School Prince," and he got into a fight for me the first night that we met. I called all my girlfriends and told them I'd met my knight in shining armor. I'd known him for thirty minutes, but I called my best friend that night and said, "I'm gonna marry this guy." He seemed to be absolutely perfect. Now that I think back on it, it's one of those things if I knew then what I know now, I could have picked up on some things.

These types of fantasies are common to both sexes. Mack is a high school senior, the captain of his varsity wrestling squad. He came into treatment after assaulting a girl he had broken up with. He relates some of the expectations he held about dating before he got started.

> I was like, you know, lookin' for "a babe." I guess I was trying to get approval from other guys, 'cause my friends all talked about going out with girls, and I wasn't yet. I was spending most of my time practicing with the team, working out. I guess looks were really important, because I was spending time

every day trying to improve my body. I wanted to date someone who felt the same way. I'd fantasize a lot while I was working on free weights, and had a pretty good idea what the perfect girl should look like, what kind of reaction I'd get from guys at school when they saw us together, stuff like that. In my fantasy she was, like, perfect. She wanted to go everywhere I wanted to go, do things I wanted to do. I really thought it would be, like, no hassle. It was just a question of finding the right girl and—bam—it would just happen.

It's clear from what Linda and Mack are saying that, long before people start dating, they have a clear idea of the kind of person they want to be with. They construct in their minds a list of desirable features, collected from early experiences with and images of the opposite sex. These images may include movie and recording artists, other "cultural icons" (anybody whose poster gets hung in your room), and even teachers and parents. Most young people could probably describe in great detail the physical traits or attitudes of that "special someone." Out of this kind of thinking comes the myth that there is a "special someone" for each one of us, a perfect complement, someone who longs just to make us happy.

THE "SPECIAL SOMEONE"

In the study of human psychology, the picture we construct of the perfect female person is referred to by the Latin word *anima;* the perfect male person by the word *animus.* Psychologists believe that we attach to that image all those characteristics we have difficulty accepting, or owning, about ourselves.

For example, if a young woman feels weaker than those around her, her "special someone," or *animus,* may be very powerful. A young man told from early childhood not to be sensitive or submissive in any situation will project those traits onto the person he's looking for. The more his personality has been repressed, the more desperate he becomes to find his *anima,* who possesses those aspects missing in himself.

Although no one exists who perfectly matches our idea of the "special someone," most of us continually attempt to fit real people into that image. This fantasy explains why we are sometimes so strongly attracted to people who we know little or nothing about, or why we react to strangers as if "I feel like I've known him (or her) all my life." The real person we've met reminds us of the *animus* or *anima* we have been carrying around in our imagination for years. Without realizing it, we compare all the eligible people we meet with a fantasy made up of our innermost wishes, dreams, and expectations. When we finally find a likely candidate who has enough of these desired features, bells and whistles go off. We believe that we've found our knight or our princess, the great love of our life.

This type of initial attraction is normal and operates in all romantic relationships. But before we start dating, we must first realize that no one is going to meet all our needs and expectations. Instead of comparing real people to a set of ideal standards, we need to get to know and enjoy people for who they are. To build a healthy relationship, we must learn not to demand perfection or unconditional love, but work toward acceptance and genuine affection.

Problems begin when we are unwilling to let go of the "special someone" fantasy. A person entering an abusive relationship either ignores any traits and features that don't fit in with the fantasy or assumes that all those ideal features are somehow hidden. As the partners get to know each other, the person searching for the "special someone" becomes gradually more disappointed. That's when you'll hear people say, "What happened to the person I started going out with?"

As one partner tries harder to make the other into the imaginary "special someone," the two people easily get into a struggle. Linda, for example, had difficulty getting her boyfriend, Mick, to see the difference between who she is and who he wants her to be.

> He thinks he knows me. But he hurts me because he doesn't want to know what kind of person I am. When we disagree, he tells me that I'm starting to be just like my mom. He likes some things I share with my mom, like my dark, sarcastic sense of humor, but he doesn't like what comes along with it: that I can call him on what he's doing in the middle of him doing it. He doesn't like that. He tells me I'm not being myself. It's like he doesn't want to see what I'm really like.

Along with the irrational belief that such a "special someone" exists comes the fear he or she might never be found. As young people see their gangs of friends,

once mostly separated into groups of girls and boys, merging into a coed group and gradually breaking off into couples, that fear increases. It's like playing musical chairs: No one wants to be the last one left when the music stops, only to find all the potential partners have been taken. When thinking clearly, we know that there are plenty of eligible people to date, even in our little corner of the planet. But much of what drives our dating behavior is based on childhood fears. And nothing frightens us more as children than being left out.

SELF-ESTEEM AND MIXED MESSAGES

Many people who are at risk for dating violence fear being passed over in the dating dance because of some imagined flaw or imperfection in themselves. The most common trait of abused teens and of teens who abuse others is a lack of self-worth. They have a hard time accepting themselves as worthwhile, often due to messages conveyed by unthinking parents or others. As Linda explained:

> Whenever I dated guys, when I was treated well, for some reason I didn't want to be with them. It didn't feel right. It felt like there was something wrong with that guy, like he was weird, because it didn't happen very often that someone was nice to me. Mick was the first guy who I felt treated me with respect. But I had nightmares where I'd wake up in the middle of the night screaming because I thought that it was all going to end—that he didn't care about me.

Marja is a very attractive young woman who grew up in a strict Polish Catholic home. She is nineteen and married, but remembers feeling very insecure about ever getting a date.

> My folks really discouraged me from going out all through high school. I thought they knew something about me that I didn't. I was sure they were protecting me from disappointment. I remember spending nights crying my eyes out because I wasn't pretty enough, or skinny enough, or whatever. I was convinced that no boy would ever ask me out, that I was going to die a virgin and it was all my fault.

Every day we are bombarded with distorted images of reality: in movies, on television, in magazines, and in advertisements. These images are created with actors or models who do not represent the rest of us physically, with expensive clothes, makeup, and surroundings that give the impression of wealth or power, and with elaborate lighting, editing, and even computer manipulation of images to remove any imperfections. It is impossible to view these images as often as we do and not begin to believe they represent how our world is supposed to look.

Our idea of the perfect partner becomes a barrier to knowing and enjoying the people in our lives. Even more destructive is the barrier that media images create to accepting ourselves and our own worth. It is difficult to compare ourselves with those people on the page or on the screen and not feel somehow lacking.

There is no need to compare ourselves with anyone else, however. Dating is not a competitive sport. There is no winning or losing. If we're in healthy relationships, even the mistakes can be fun. If we believe that dating is a contest, we set ourselves up for the anxiety and pressure that come from fear of failure. Healthy dating starts when we learn to value ourselves, remove the pressure to compete, and accept our reality for what it is, not what we have been led to believe it is supposed to be.

Each one of us is just about perfect. We can make some bad choices, but that's simply a problem with our thinking or our behavior, which we can change. Remember that while that "special someone" does not exist, there are lots of interesting and worthwhile people who want to have a good, fun, and loving relationship just as much as you do. It takes believing in yourself, some hard work, and lots of patience to build trust, commitment, and intimacy with another person. Only in a fantasy—or on TV—is intimacy quick and easy.

FAMILY PATTERNS

Dating is like a bridge. It takes us from the family we grew up with, our "family of origin," to the start of a new family, the one we will create when we and a partner both decide that we're ready to make that commitment. Because of the time spent with our family, it becomes a powerful model for both our "family of destination" and the steps we take to get there.

Marja, who is now in an abusive marriage, realized the effect her father had on her growing up. "It wasn't until I was married that I found out that no one asked me out 'cause they were afraid of my father. He ran our house with an iron hand, and in our small Polish neighborhood his tirades were common knowledge."

Linda wished that she "could have picked up on some things" when she first met her boyfriend, Mick. Here she tells us some of those things she thinks she missed:

> I knew that a man, more than likely, is gonna be like his father. I knew that going into it, but I chose to ignore it because I don't like his father. His parents are strictly "the father is the head of the household, makes all decisions, all rules." Double standard everything. I didn't like that, didn't agree with that. Mick told me he wasn't like that. But he is.

The most powerful influence on dating behavior comes from our family of origin. The significant people in our lives while we're growing up—our parents, older sisters and brothers, other family members in the home— shape the expectations we have about the opposite sex and about ourselves, and some of the roles we will play as we try to fit into the complex ritual of dating. The different types of people who end up in abusive relationships often have similar family backgrounds.

Here are a few of the common experiences of those who are at risk for dating violence:

- alcohol or drug use in the family of origin
- witnessing the abuse of one parent by the other
- physical or verbal abuse of a child in the family
- traditional or "rigid" beliefs about the roles of men and women

- a negative family attitude toward women
- lack of approval or abandonment by a parent
- resolution of family conflicts by having a "winner" and a "loser"

The presence of some or all of these factors in a family does not guarantee that the members will eventually be abused or will abuse someone else. It does mean, however, that the family members have lived in an environment where these attitudes or behaviors were considered "normal." To survive, often they had to screen out some of the painful reality, or simply believe that all families lived the same way. It may be harder for these people in later life to recognize the danger signs in a partner's behavior or problems in their own.

As you will see from the stories in this book, change is always possible. No one has to stay in a relationship that is stifling or painful. Each of us can update the myths about dating that we have inherited from childhood. We can build self-esteem by meeting our own needs, not the expectations of others. We can change old rules and messages that don't work for us. And we can make dating safer and more fun. All the influences from our past stay right there—in the past—unless we choose to bring them into the present. Dating is a bridge, stretching into a future that we create. The better our choices and behavior while we are dating, the better that future will be.

CHAPTER TWO

THE DATING DANCE BEGINS

There were things about him I didn't know at first. Mick tried to prove to me that he was open-minded, and that's what I saw. I've found out since he isn't that way. He won't come out and say this, but he believes that a woman is supposed to be meek and mild and stay in her place. Now if you ask him, he'll say "No, I believe everything should be fifty/fifty." But that's not the way he behaves. — Linda

When we meet someone we like, we experience the rush that comes from getting to know new people and becoming aware of their interest in us. We respond to this situation by trying to get noticed, letting the other persons know we like them and trying to make them like us, too. In all the excitement, it's hard to see that we are developing patterns of thinking and behaving that will last throughout the entire relationship.

Rules get set in the beginning of a relationship—about honesty, the roles each person will play, and how free the partners are to be their real selves. In a healthy dating relationship, feelings can be expressed and these rules discussed, which ensures that both partners will be able to play by roughly the same rules, and their roles will be equal and flexible. In an abusive dating relationship, these rules are not communicated out loud, but in subtle messages and nonverbal cues. The roles are more narrow, and the choices for each partner are different and unequal. How do we present ourselves to a potential dating partner?

MATCHING

Let's say you've met someone you're attracted to, and you think that he or she might also be attracted to you. To keep this new and fragile relationship going, each person needs to fulfill some of the other's expectations. This is common to all relationships. In healthy dating, we each reveal something about ourselves, and hope that the other person is satisfied with who we are. But what happens when we become involved with someone who we believe may be our "knight" or "princess?" Can we risk disappointing that person and letting him or her get away?

The fear of losing our "special someone" keeps us guarded about our real selves, hiding parts of our personality and sometimes pretending to be what we're not. This process is called *matching*. To fulfill the expectations of our new partner, we put our own personality "on hold" while trying to match what we think the other person's idea is of who we should be.

Mack describes trying to impress a potential dating partner:

> So I meet this girl, right, at a party I'm at with some other guys on the team. I've been clued in that she likes me by my best friend's girlfriend, so I check

> her out and decide she's pretty cute. I thought I'd
> be tough, so I start slammin' back shots of
> schnapps. Later, I think I asked to drive her home.
> She said yes, but I found out later she was afraid
> we'd have a wreck on the way. She didn't say any-
> thing about it to me, at least that I can remember.

Leanne, a sixteen-year-old keyboard player for a heavy metal band, talks about her attempts to match her boyfriend's expectations when they began to date.

> I was fifteen when I first started going out with
> Steve. It just seemed natural to be around each
> other all the time. I stopped hanging out with my
> friends, or with the other guys in the band, even. It
> meant so much to me to have this guy giving all
> his attention to me. I was afraid that if I ever said I
> wasn't available, I'd blow it. I didn't notice the
> friends I was losing, 'cause I just figured this was
> part of falling in love and growing up.

In a healthy relationship, when we become more inti-mate with our partner, we reveal more of our feelings and personality. We balance the expectations of our partner with our own need to maintain our identity. By doing this, we attract people who appreciate our au-thentic self, and there is no need for deception.

In an unhealthy relationship based on matching the expectations of our partner, the opposite takes place. We lose more of our real self as we get more involved with a partner. There may be some rewards, but the person who is getting attention and affection is the per-son we are only pretending to be. The real self, the one that is hiding, has needs and feelings that are not being met and feels unloved and unappreciated.

It's not easy pretending to be what we're not. Creating this deception causes tension, because we are always in fear of being found out. We may start to resent the person we are trying to please—and sometimes this can even lead to violence.

It can be disappointing if a potential partner does not seem to accept who you are. But rather than waste time and energy pretending to be someone or something that you're not, it's healthier to accept the fact and to continue the search for someone who will appreciate you.

ACCOMMODATION

Matching is the process of transforming ourselves into our partner's fantasy. Accommodation is the process of transforming a partner into our fantasy. It prevents us from seeing those attitudes or behaviors that don't fit the idealized image we have of a dating partner. We ignore important details about the real person we're with, and persist in seeing only our "special someone."

Marja explains her attempts to accommodate her partner's behavior when they first began going out:

> I really wasn't happy going out with Dick, but I was so grateful there was someone who could rescue me from the unhappiness in my family that I saw only those things about him that I could love: his constancy, his strength. All the rest I ignored: his bullying, showing me off like a trophy in front of

his friends, the names he'd sometimes call me. I endured all that because I refused to see that I'd set myself up to go from one terrible situation to another.

When we're swept up in the magic of a new romance, we resist those things that will bring us back down to earth. The more we cling to the "storybook" relationship, the less important we consider those details that don't fit the fantasy. We won't risk expressing dissatisfaction with our partner's attitude or behavior because we are afraid this will somehow spoil the magic of our budding relationship.

By accommodating our partner's behavior, we put up with things we don't like. For example, many people tolerate a partner's drinking, or let themselves be bossed around. They can't admit that the real person they are getting to know is not the "knight" or "princess" they first imagined. Because these feelings of disappointment are either ignored or not expressed, there is no chance the situation will improve.

Steve recalls the difficulty he had in the early stages of his relationship with Leanne:

When she started playing metal, all the other guys in her band were much older, and most of them got high. She would come back from rehearsal pretty wasted some times. Once we went out after a band practice, and Leanne sort of stumbled every time she got up from her chair. I was embarrassed, but didn't let on. I just held it inside because I was so afraid that if I complained, we wouldn't be going out any more. And being with her meant a lot to me.

When we accommodate, we have no way to deal with hurts and resentments, so they build up below the surface. These shut-down feelings rob us of energy, which explains the fatigue that some people experience when they are in an abusive dating relationship. But problems that are not communicated to a partner cannot be resolved. If we can't even admit the problems to ourselves, we often end up in conflict with friends and family who express concern over what they see is going on. This conflict then causes people in abusive relationships to become more isolated from outside support, which puts them at greater risk for further abuse.

For any of our relationships to work, we have to be able to express our feelings, even the uncomfortable ones. We need to be able to give, and receive, to make the relationship grow. In a healthy relationship, we are free to express reservations about a partner's attitudes or behavior. If the other person can listen and respond to a partner's feelings, each finds out more about the other. This gradual awareness of one's self and one's partner is part of the adventure of a healthy dating relationship.

STEREOTYPING

We all are capable of the full range of human emotions: from deepest grief to highest joy; from worthlessness and despair to self-satisfaction and competence; from panic to serenity. But traditions, family messages, and other social pressures begin in earliest childhood to shape us into expressing those emotions with a narrow range of acceptable behaviors. Depending on whether we are male or female, certain "sex-typed" behaviors are selectively rewarded or punished.

For example, a small boy has his football stolen and comes home crying. His "traditional male" dad says, "You kick that kid's butt and get your football back, or you'll get two beatings: one from him and one from me." But if his twin sister beats up a girl for swiping her Barbie, the same parent says, "Now, now, we musn't hit our friends. Go and say you're sorry, and let her play with your doll." These are gross exaggerations. Actually, much of this conditioning is subtle, conveyed in the different toys, games, teams, even musical instruments available to male and female children. But the effect of this conditioning is to give girls and boys very different rules about who they are and how they should respond to certain situations. Gradually, children learn to feel comfortable expressing certain emotions, while failing to recognize others or being taught to control them.

When these children reach adolescence, there is intense pressure to form an adult identity and gain acceptance from others. When thrown into the dating dance, the fear that "everyone else will find a partner except me" prompts members of both sexes to look for ways to appear competent and secure, especially to potential dating partners. They do this by exaggerating those behaviors they have been taught are associated with people of their gender.

This process, called *stereotyping,* squeezes the full range of human response into a small range of attitudes, emotions, and behaviors. Whereas identity is unique to each person and flexible to different situations, stereotypes are rigid, appearing at times like cartoon characters. People impose sexual stereotypes on themselves to become more visible—and more attractive, they believe—to the opposite sex. They may act out the role of the tough, rebellious male, for example, or the passive, flirtatious female.

Leanne remembers her first fantasies about dating:

> When I was younger, all the girls used to sleep over at my house. We'd stay up and talk about boys and just giggle. None of us were into the "straight" guys, the ones who got high marks or were in clubs. I remember that we would all drool over the kind of guys who had that attitude, who seemed so sure of themselves, the "wild ones" who were always getting into trouble.

The boy who plays the macho role of always being in control, or becomes stereotyped as a "jock," ceases to be a whole person. The girl who focuses on pleasing others loses touch with her own likes and dislikes. When these two "types" start dating each other, they set up a pattern in which it is normal for the male to make all the choices—about dinner, films, sex—and for the female to hide her real feelings or opinions and just "go along." Often the girl feels grateful for this attention and what she perceives as "protection," and submits to her partner's wishes in all areas of their relationship.

This was Marja's first dating experience with the young man she later married:

> I can't really remember why I finally said I'd go out with Dick. He had asked me again and again and I always said, "No." He was older, kind of a tough guy, and I think I was a little frightened of him. But he was persistent, he just wouldn't take no for an answer. He wore me down until I said yes. He came over, I got in his car, and out we went. He never asked me where I wanted to go, nothing. I wasn't sure I liked it, but I didn't really know how to get out of seeing him again. We'd get home, and my father would be waiting up, this scowl on his face. I couldn't tell my father I didn't like it. I was afraid if I did he would never let me go out again.

When a young man's "role" is to make all those choices and his partner's "role" is to passively go along, the power in that relationship is not distributed equally. She does all the "giving," he does all the "taking." Occasionally these roles are reversed, and the female makes all the choices in the relationship, with a similar outcome. The same pattern can also occur in romantic relationships between people of the same sex. Both people are locked into a role, either dominant or submissive, that keeps them from learning more about their partners or themselves.

Another consequence of stereotyping is that neither partner sees the other as a whole person with unique feelings, wishes, and desires. They begin to view each other more and more as objects whose sole purpose is to satisfy their needs. The term "sex object" refers to a person who is considered and treated as if his or her only role is sexual. At the core of sexual harassment and sexual abuse is the belief that the victim doesn't have an identity and is without feelings or needs.

In a healthy relationship, the partners have an equal say when deciding how much time they spend together, who they hang out with, what their recreational activities are, and what their level of physical intimacy is. Without this healthy balance of power, the relationship is no longer an opportunity for growth for either partner, which is what dating should be about.

When we limit ourselves to only a small range of attitudes, emotions, and behaviors, we sacrifice our need for acceptance, for self-expression, and for a strong sense of identity and self-worth. These unfulfilled needs don't go away. Instead they feed our fantasy that some partner will be able to perfectly and effortlessly satisfy all these needs and make us whole again. This sets up a power struggle between our expectations and the expectations of the partner, so we begin to play "Who's the boss?"

CHAPTER THREE
WHO'S THE BOSS?

When he left for basic training, he made these rules. He didn't want me to go to clubs and bars. He'd say, "I trust myself totally, I'm just afraid of what you would do without me." I went along with that for a couple of months, and then I decided, "That's crazy." I knew I could go out with my girlfriends, and that I wouldn't go out on him. So I'd tell him when I went out, I never lied to him. We stayed together, but we argued and fought about the whole rules thing. It was a big fiasco. — Linda

In a healthy relationship, as we get to know our partner, we should gradually realize that he or she is not our "special someone," but a living, growing, independent human being. We can then deepen our connection with and respect for that person and build the relationship from there.

In an unhealthy relationship, one partner cannot give up the fantasy that the other will meet all expectations. That partner starts to force the other into becoming that "special someone." This sets up an emotional tug-of-war, which replaces intimacy and cooperation with a struggle for power and control.

POWER AND CONTROL

The struggle for control in a dating relationship begins in subtle ways. First there are assumptions that different options or rules apply to each partner, based on gender or who has more money, for example. One partner may spread rumors or habitually lie, which keeps the other in the dark about what's really going on. A jealous person may subject a partner to a high level of suspicion and scrutiny, denying the right to privacy or access to friends outside the relationship. Or by cheating, one person gives the strong message that he or she has little respect for, or commitment to, the partner.

This is Linda's story about her partner's attempt to gain control:

> I know there was some jealousy on his part, which is why he wanted to keep me from going out on my own. I think he didn't trust himself. I came to find out months later that he was drinking and partying, and lying about it the whole time. He'd let slip little things, like he'd say, "We went into the city one night to this place." And I'd say, "You never told me you went there. Who were you with?" He felt like he had to keep secrets from me, like I was going to get mad at him. I just wanted him to be honest.

These forms of controlling a partner's behavior ensure that the needs or expectations of one partner come first. That person gains an unfair advantage by making the partner feel powerless.

Leanne recalls the first argument she had with her boyfriend, Steve. He used the tactic of withholding attention and ignoring her to get his way:

> It was pretty silly, really, just about what movie we were going to that night. When I said I wanted to go to a different movie than the one he suggested, he just got real quiet. That night, we got to the theatre and he just bought the tickets to his movie, like I hadn't said anything. Then he gave me the cold shoulder the whole rest of the night.

The struggle for power and control is where dating violence begins, with its manipulation, "wearing down" of opposition, and intimidation. One partner often submits, frightened by the threatening idea: "If you don't, you lose the great love of your life." Or the injured partner may retaliate, using similar tactics in an attempt to gain control. Either way, the relationship has crossed the line between healthy dating and potential dating violence.

THE CYCLE OF VIOLENCE

One reason dating abuse is hard to recognize is that no relationship is violent all the time. Even relationships that ended when one partner murdered the other had periods of calm and affection. There were also, however, periods when tension was unbearably thick and then sudden explosions when one or both partners lashed out verbally and physically. This is the cycle of violence, a recurring pattern common to all abusive dating relationships. These phases follow each other in a fairly regular pattern that repeats itself, over and over, in a downward spiral.

The cycle begins with the struggle for power and control, which, along with outside pressures, creates a great deal of stress upon the dating partners and their emotional resources. This is the first phase, known as the tension-building phase. Pressures build to a point where conflicts escalate into emotional or physical violence. The second phase of the cycle is the acute battering phase. This is followed by a period of remorse and reconciliation where the relationship attempts to regain harmony, leading to a period of relative calm. This makeup period is referred to as the "honeymoon" phase. Unless there is a change within the relationship or intervention from outside the relationship, this period of calm leads right into the tension-building phase, and the whole cycle repeats.

It may take months, even years, to complete this cycle the first time. But gradually the phases get shorter, and the cycle of violence begins to repeat with increasing speed. The partners begin to anticipate the different phases, and may even believe they can control what will happen next, or how much force will be used.

It's hard to tell when the cycle of violence starts. It is usually obvious first to people outside the relationship, then to one partner. By the time both partners become aware that they're trapped, patterns are in place that make it difficult to recognize the danger or the need for outside help. The cycle can be broken at any point, but the partners first must realize that they are in it.

Remember, these phases are just devices for understanding a very complex process. No relationship fits into a neat little diagram, with every piece exactly in place. In real life, the phases may overlap, reverse order, or some may be skipped entirely. But as you read, ask yourself if any of this sounds familiar. This pattern may apply to the relationship of a couple you know or to your own. Keep an open mind. There's no need to feel guilty or criticize. The first step to breaking the cycle is simply to recognize it.

PHASE ONE: TENSION BUILDING

All dating couples experience many types of stress: financial and school pressures, the difficulty of dealing with biological changes, peer pressures, decisions about education and careers, and so on. A healthy couple can help each other with these problems. But for a couple locked into a pattern of dominance and submission, there is no way of cooperating with each other. In addition, the relationship itself creates a variety of stressful situations, such as:

- trying to maintain appearances that the relationship is working
- criticism and lack of support from family members aware of what is happening in the relationship
- isolation from friends
- breakdown of communication and trust between partners
- pressure from peers to stay together despite the difficulties
- problems at school or at work as the relationship consumes more energy
- lowered self-esteem as a result of mistreatment of or by the other partner

The pressure increases over time until eventually it cannot be handled safely in that relationship, particularly if one partner tries to relieve stress with some form of violent behavior.

It is possible to break the cycle of violence and get help at this early stage, but the abused partner may believe that would be a sign of disloyalty or betrayal. He or she may be unable to break off the relationship for fear the abuse will escalate to physical battering. The abused partner may attempt to "fight back" and retaliate by attempting to see someone else, which feeds the mounting tension. As the power struggle escalates, the dominant partner may try even harder to take back control and get the fantasy back.

Linda describes her experience:

> I've been scared, I've been afraid to release my feelings because I was afraid that he would hurt me. I can talk in a normal tone of voice, but if I yell at him, he'll get in my face. See, he can sit there and yell at me, but if I get in his face, he says, "Who do you think you are screaming at me?" That's what I'm scared of, there's just no talking to him. I can see another fight coming, so I just shut up and don't deal with it.

As it gets harder and harder to see our partner as the willing, accommodating "special someone," the fantasy dies. And with that loss comes the fear that we have been betrayed.

JEALOUSY

Possessiveness, or jealousy, although it is a normal human response, is sometimes used as an emotional weapon and as a justification for depriving people of their privacy. Sadly, jealousy is often misinterpreted as a sign of love.

Cyndi, sixteen years old and pregnant, talks about her boyfriend's jealousy:

> People are tellin' me that slavery is dead, but unh-unh. Kevin wants me to follow him around like a shadow. If I look at somebody, not even like flirting, he's all, "Where you been, who was that you were talkin' to?" All macho and stuff. One time he accused me of carryin' someone else's baby, even though he knows it's his. He says he does that third degree because he loves me. I don't think so, it doesn't feel like love.

Jealousy is not a sign of love. It is a sign of fear that the "object" of desire will be lost. Usually it has nothing to do with the person being possessed, or whether that person is actually flirting or is attracted to others. Instead it reveals aspects of the jealous person's personality. The first is low self-worth.

After some months in therapy, Kevin was able to identify what was behind his jealous rages toward his live-in girlfriend:

> I couldn't shake the feeling that I was a nobody, that Cyndi couldn't possibly love a screw-up like me. I was afraid that she would leave with the first guy who walked by. Anyone had to be better than me. I figured if I could hound her enough before it happened, or scare her too much to look at anyone else, she wouldn't be able to leave me.

Unrealistic expectations about a partner's behavior are often the cause of jealousy. It's impossible and unfair to expect a dating partner to have no contact with friends or family members, or to never express positive feelings toward others.

Most jealous people have been abandoned or hurt at some time in their past. The pain of loss is very real, and the jealous person will do anything to prevent those bad feelings from striking again. To prevent another loss, the jealous partner will try to keep the partner from noticing anyone else, or will isolate the partner so no one will notice her or him.

Steve, who lost his mother when he was young, had a strong reaction when watching his girlfriend's band perform:

> It should have made me happy: there was Leanne, playing the crap out of her keyboards, people screaming like it was Metallica or something. But I was miserable, I wanted to drag her out of there, away from all those people looking at her. After her gig, when we were alone, I'd get distant. I had a totally bad attitude. I figured that if any guy at the club wanted to take her home, she would do it sooner or later. I wanted to punish her for that. I knew that Leanne had feelings for me, but I just didn't want to see it.

Another myth about jealousy is that it will end when two people get married or move in together. In reality, the opposite is true. To a jealous person, greater commitment only strengthens the belief that the partner is a possession, and often increases the emotional dependence and need for control. There are no quick fixes for jealousy, and no change is possible until the jealous person stops blaming the partner and begins to take responsibility for his or her own feelings.

We need to ask ourselves whether our fears about what a partner will do are real or just imagined. It helps to talk to our partner or someone we trust outside the relationship. When we have a better understanding of reality and our own feelings, as well as more open, honest communication with a partner, it is less likely that we'll react jealously for no reason.

COMMUNICATION

The greatest joys of any relationship are the thoughts and feelings shared by two people. Part of the pleasure of any shared experience—listening to music or watching films—is letting someone else know how it makes us feel. This is true even of a difficult experience, which becomes more bearable if we can let off steam with someone who's been through it with us. By listening to and respecting what our partners are saying, we get insight into their needs and wants, and an opportunity to grow even closer.

When two people are dating, communication is essential in dealing with conflicts or problems that arise. It acts as an escape valve to release the tensions inside and pressures outside the relationship. When discussing differences of opinion, communication helps us find a middle ground, so we can create a solution where both partners win, even if they can't get their own way.

Conflict is a normal part of any healthy relationship. The belief that a happy couple never disagrees is just a myth. Conflicts may start around issues as simple as "What movie do we see tonight" or as complicated as "Should we have sex?"

In a healthy relationship, the partners resolve conflicts with mutual respect and equality of power, which means that each side has an equal chance of getting his or her way. Through honest communication, the couple can reach a compromise that both people are comfortable with. Conflicts help us to stretch our boundaries and can actually increase our commitment to a relationship, but only if they are resolved through a process of discussion and negotiating—which we'll call "fighting fair."

In abusive relationships, conflicts are present but are not resolved. Usually one person uses emotional manipulation or threats of violence to control the other person and get his or her own way. This is "fighting unfair."

Here are some guidelines for identifying fair and unfair fighting when conflict arises. Ask yourself which rules you follow when dealing with a conflict with your dating partner. Do you fight fair or unfair? Remember, you can't force someone to play by the rules, but you can decide whether or not you want to be dating someone who won't play fair.

FAIR

Schedule an appropriate time and place to discuss and negotiate the issues.

Deal with one issue at a time. Keep the focus on the present situation.

Focus on the issue, the attitude, or behavior that's creating the conflict.

Take turns talking.

Be sure you and your partner each have an equal amount of time to speak.

Be specific when asking for what you want.

Listen carefully to what is being said, and always ask your partner to explain if you are unclear about what he or she means.

Focus on finding solutions, and be willing to compromise.

Try to reinforce what is working and positive in the relationship.

Don't forget to laugh once in a while.

UNFAIR

Avoid the conflict entirely or bring up the issue without warning at inappropriate times.

Shift from one issue to another and bring up unresolved past conflicts.

Focus on the other person, use name-calling and blaming to intimidate and attack.

Try to do all the talking.

Tell your side of the story, then tell your partner's side of the story.

Expect your partner to be able to read your mind.

Don't listen when your partner is talking. Instead plan what you will say when you get your chance. Interrupt.

Keep insisting, "It's my way or no way." Insult or criticize the other person when he or she doesn't give in.

Stay focused on what's wrong and, most important, on who is responsible.

Treat every conflict like it's the end of the world.

But what happens when communication isn't working? What if one partner refuses to listen or even to see the real person that he or she is in the relationship with? Linda describes her frustration at trying to communicate with her boyfriend after their unsuccessful attempt to deal with a conflict.

> I try to talk about it later, and there's just no talking to him. I can see another argument coming, so I just don't deal with it then. It's hard for me to remember what the problem was about, because when you're in a rage you don't remember very well. It's easier to make like it never happened, or just drop the whole thing. So I don't bother, I just shut down.

When communication breaks down, discussion turns into a yelling match where each partner struggles to be heard, usually pouring out blame and accusation. Both partners have to justify their feelings, because each is being judged by the other as wrong.

Tension, jealousy, and lack of communication destroy the trust and commitment between two people. In a healthy relationship, there are ways to work through these problems through efforts at increased self-awareness and understanding as well as through counseling. In an unhealthy and abusive relationship, this breakdown sets up the next phase of the cycle of violence—the acute battering phase.

CHAPTER FOUR
WHEN VIOLENCE BEGINS

He's never come out and hit me—well yeah, he has. He slapped me one time. He's hurt me many other times, though. One time he came up to me when I was on my grandma's steps, and he took my wrist and just twisted it back. And then pushed me up against the wall so hard, I mean, it made a bruise right here on my arm. — Linda

What is dating violence? Because we are surrounded by the depiction of many violent acts in films and on TV, and hear about so much violence in the news, it's sometimes hard to identify what is violent behavior and what isn't. And it often doesn't seem real even when it's happening right in front of us.

A clue to what constitutes dating violence is what it does to a person, or what the abusive partner intends for it to do. The goal of violence is to control someone else—to determine what that person will do or feel.

In a healthy relationship, being assertive—making choices for ourselves, communicating our feelings or wants to our partner—increases communication and prevents power struggles by balancing the wants and needs of both partners. When one partner becomes aggressive, however—making choices for the other, controlling what that partner can or can't do and say—the relationship is abusive.

Physical injury is only the most obvious part of an unsafe or abusive dating relationship. Dating violence occurs whenever words or actions are used to control someone else's behavior.

THE FOUR TYPES
OF DATING VIOLENCE

For the purposes of discussion, we'll separate dating violence into four types: physical abuse, emotional abuse, sexual abuse, and the destruction of property or pets. In reality, however, incidents of dating abuse often fall in two or more of these categories, and there is no clear separation.

Physical abuse includes punching, slapping, biting, arm twisting, holding someone down, any use of a weapon or threatening with one, or putting someone in a situation where he or she is at risk for harm. Driving recklessly or threatening to push someone from a moving car are forms of physical abuse (a motor vehicle can be a deadly weapon). Physical abuse also includes any threat to harm a partner or to commit suicide.

Michelle describes a violent incident in a recent dating relationship:

> One night he was taking me home. He had a test the next day so he was kinda irritable. We'd been bickering all night. We were driving and I said something smart, and he jerked off the road in the

> middle of nowhere in the pitch black. I had no idea where we were or what was happening. I was sure we were having a wreck. He just scared the hell out of me.

Emotional abuse consists of sarcasm, accusations, nagging, shouting, insults, crying, threatening, withholding affection, or lying. It also includes revenge, or "punishing" a dating partner for not getting one's way, by obnoxious or drunken behavior, expressing attraction for others, or criticism of a partner's family and friends. Because so much emotional abuse consists of words used in a harmful way, it is often called verbal abuse.

Sexual abuse includes any forced sexual activity, that is, anything a partner has not consented to or has asked to stop doing after initially consenting. It also includes put-downs and demeaning remarks about a partner's gender, body, clothing, or previous dating behavior. Because sexual abuse affects the most private part of one's life, it can damage a partner's self-esteem and sense of security. It is not uncommon for a victim of sexual abuse to have lasting emotional distress and great difficulty establishing trust and intimacy in later relationships.

Michelle was a victim of verbal and sexual abuse from her partner soon after they became engaged:

> Right after I accepted, the abuse started. Because I'd dated guys before, that's what I got crap for more than anything else. He'd say, "You're a slut, you're a whore. Nobody's gonna love you except me." It didn't matter that I never slept with any of them.

This entire book is designed to help you answer that, but it is helpful to have a checklist of some of the most common warning signs. Answer these questions about yourself and your dating partner as honestly as possible:

1. Are you belittled for giving your opinion, or are your feelings not taken seriously?
2. Are you often criticized by your dating partner, especially about your appearance or behavior, and sometimes in front of others?
3. Does your partner lie to you repeatedly, or react angrily when confronted about lying?
4. Does your partner order you instead of ask, or make all the decisions for both of you without your input?
5. Does your partner set rules for your behavior, like who you can and can't see, or what you are supposed to wear?
6. Is your partner jealous or possessive, constantly checking up on where you are and what you are doing?
7. Does your partner prevent you from spending as much time with your family or friends as you would like?
8. Have you ever been blamed by your partner for mistakes he or she has made? Have you ever been told that it was your own fault that you were being mistreated?
9. Have you ever felt pressured to have sex or forced to go further than you wanted to when making out?
10. Does your partner show disrespect for you or appear to have a personality change when using drugs or alcohol?

11. Are you ever frightened by your partner's behavior, explosive temper, or sudden mood
swings?
12. Have you ever been threatened with either
physical violence or a weapon by your dating partner?
13. Has your partner ever been violent toward
any other dating partner? Does he or she
blame past partners for all the problems in
those relationships?
14. Does your partner display extreme jealousy
when you talk to others or express warm feelings for anyone else?
15. Has your partner ever said that he or she
could not live without you or would rather kill
you than see you with anyone else?
16. Does your partner refuse to break up or
threaten to commit suicide or harm you in
some way if you try to break up?

If you answered yes to any of these questions,
there may be some emotional or physical abuse
in your relationship—and the potential for further
abuse. These questions are not meant to predict
the future but to make you think about what kind
of relationship you are in. Think of it this way:
None of the behaviors described above takes
place in a healthy relationship. You deserve to
date without worrying about your safety and to
choose a happy and healthy relationship.

If you answered yes to any of these questions, please talk to someone you trust and check
it out. It doesn't hurt to ask about a problem, only
to ignore it. Or check the Sources for Help and
Information section at the back of the book.

Sometimes personal property is damaged as a way of manipulating a dating partner. Breaking a gift from someone, smashing a car windshield, slashing tires, and threatening to harm a partner's pet are all abusive tactics that use an object as a substitute for the real target of the violence. Sometimes an abusive partner will destroy his or her own possessions along with, or instead of, the intended victim's. Because this type of assault is not directed at its intended victim, it is often mistaken simply as an outburst of temper or a release of tension. But the intention is clear: "I get my way or you're next."

PHASE TWO: ACUTE BATTERING

In an unhealthy relationship, in the first phase of the cycle of violence, tension builds to an explosive point. Attempts by both partners to reduce tension fail. The push to maintain power and control in the relationship increases until one partner pushes too hard. It's like a stuck water faucet—when it doesn't turn off, you turn it harder, then harder, until something finally gives.

Compromise, the sharing of decisions, and the alternating of who gets whose way are all methods of dealing with the tensions that naturally arise in a healthy dating relationship. But these options are not available to a couple locked in a struggle where there has to be a winner and a loser. Instead the partners often feel trapped in the relationship, due to misguided notions of loyalty and love, or the belief that they cannot attract other, healthier partners. The tension and frustration grow until one or both partners lash out aggressively in an attempt to take control. If one of the partners becomes abusive, this lashing-out is an acute battering incident, the phase in the cycle of violence where the most apparent abuse takes place.

Kevin describes his assault on his girlfriend, for which he was arrested:

> I don't remember much, I just sort of blacked out, I was so angry. And so drunk. They accused me of sexual assault because I bit her, but I wasn't trying to rape her. I just wanted to shut her up.

There are natural restraints that keep people from hurting each other: an aversion to inflicting pain, awareness of the feelings of others, fear of getting caught. But empathy and the fear of consequences are part of our "higher mind" functions, which are either impaired or fast asleep when we are high or drunk. The majority of assaults, especially the first time they occur in a dating relationship, happen when the batterer is intoxicated.

Because it releases tension and gives the aggressive partner control, violence appears to settle the immediate conflict that set off the acute battering incident. The abuser may not even feel at fault and instead may blame the partner, the partner's bad attitude, or the intoxication. Such a person often will apologize immediately, promising that it will never happen again. But without suffering meaningful consequences for the violent behavior, such as arrest or loss of the relationship, the abuser is likely to act out again. For couples that do not break up following the acute battering incident, the relationship continues to the third phase of the cycle of violence—the "honeymoon."

DENIAL AND MINIMIZATION

Following a battering incident, both the abuser and the victim are overwhelmed with feelings of loss. Trust and intimacy have been shattered and are replaced by shame and fear. One or both partners may attempt to separate themselves from the painful reality through denial. Denial is the refusal to believe the abusive incident occurred or that it was meant to be harmful.

Cyndi explained to her best friend why she put up with emotional abuse by her boyfriend:

> I tried to tell my friend Tami that everybody gets in fights, not just me and Kevin. He didn't, like, physically abuse me. That time my mother says I was bit on the leg we were just horsing around. I cried and stuff, but he can really be so sweet.

Another defense, called minimization, attempts to make the battering incident seem less violent or important. When minimizing violence, the words "just" and "only" are often used, as they were when Linda attempted to confront her boyfriend's denial about physical abuse:

> I said, "Mick, you hurt me. You could have broken my wrist." And he denied it. "I just held your arm like this." There's a difference between holding somebody's arm and leaving a bruise. Even when I showed it to him, he's like, "Well, I don't know what happened. I don't know where you got that." He doesn't think that he's abused me at all.

Denial and minimization are forms of self-defense that keep us from realizing how shocked or afraid we are as a result of the abuse. An abused partner may sincerely want to believe that this was the only time violence would occur, and that the hitting and hurting will end. But when victims are stuck in denial, they are not being honest with themselves or with friends or family who may express concern. They then become more isolated, which increases the risk for further abuse.

ISOLATION

Both partners in an abusive incident usually feel shame after the assault, and avoid talking to others about it for fear of embarrassment and criticism. Family and friends may withdraw because they feel uncomfortable or helpless or disgusted by what they see going on. The partners become more dependent upon each other for approval and companionship.

Cyndi described the level of isolation in her relationship with Kevin:

> When we're around each other, everything is fine. I only wish everybody would leave us alone: my mother, the courts. No one understands what it's really like when it's just the two of us. I don't want to give him up.

Dating violence usually happens in private. Often, there are no witnesses to an acute battering incident. The abuser may fear the consequences if others know of the assault, and so denies that it happened and tries to keep it secret. Victims are often threatened that the abuse will get worse if they tell, or they are prevented from communicating with others.

This is why traditional counseling often can't break the cycle of violence. There is so much pressure on both partners to keep the abuse secret that it rarely comes up as an issue in discussion of their relationship. And because counseling can provide a false sense of security, it puts both partners at risk for continued violence. No counseling is effective for dating violence unless it focuses on the victim's safety, confronts the issue of denial, and connects both partners to ongoing support to overcome their isolation.

A BAD TEMPER

We all learn very early in life that we are responsible for how we treat other people. But many people ignore this lesson, treat others unfairly, and get away with it by claiming they have bad tempers. We hear the same thing from those who are mistreated by them, who make sure to warn us of his or her unpredictable, explosive, and totally unavoidable responses. These victims are busy apologizing for making their partners mad, "setting them off," or "pushing their buttons." They fail to realize that the abusive partner is the one reponsible for his or her own actions. There is no excuse for abusive behavior.

Mick, Linda's boyfriend, holds her responsible for his feelings and how he chooses to respond to them.

> I snap when she starts pushing my buttons. I wish I could control my anger, but she won't let me get away. She follows me. I'll scream, "Get away from me. I need to be alone." I mean it. And she won't.

What does it really mean when people claim to have a bad temper? It means they have little sense of their feelings, thoughts, or identity. It means that they cannot recognize when stress has built up beyond the point where they can deal with it safely. It also means that when they finally notice what's going on, they react without thinking of the consequences. Finally, it means that someone else will be held responsible for the violent behavior.

Many people confuse a bad temper with anger. Anger is an emotion, a natural and valuable response to something going on inside or around us. Anger tells us that there is some threat or danger around us. By paying attention to the feeling and choosing a response, we can try to reduce that threat.

In a healthy relationship we can express our feelings, even feelings of anger, in a constructive way, without hurting anyone. In an unhealthy relationship, when there is a flare-up of temper, feelings that have been repressed are often expressed in a destructive and harmful way, and someone else is usually held responsible for them.

Mack blames his bad temper and his partner for his violent outbursts:

> I don't think about it when I'm doing it. I just get so angry, I don't know what I'm doing. I just have this temper. She should know that what she does sets me off.

BLAME-SHIFTING

A batterer may feel tremendous guilt after an assault. To get rid of these uncomfortable emotions, abusers create the fantasy that they are blameless for their actions. They focus on the argument that led up to the assault, and on the behavior of their partners. This is called blame-shifting. It's a way of saying, "Because you wouldn't do what I wanted, I had to hurt you."

Linda's boyfriend, Mick, blames her for his loss of control:

> I told her, "You know when I'm angry with you, and I scream at you to get away from me, I'm about to go off." I almost feel like she deserves whatever happens next for following me and just torturing me like that.

By blame-shifting, the victim of the violence is made to feel responsible for the assault. The blame is literally "shifted" from one partner to the other. This makes it hard, both for those in the relationship and those outside of it—parents, friends, and even police—to sort out what really happened and to respond appropriately to the violence.

Michelle confronted her boyfriend's blame-shifting after he frightened her by driving recklessly:

> He kept saying, "I told you I was gonna do something stupid. I warned you, but you overreacted." Like it was my fault. I said, "The only reason you think I overreacted is because I didn't respond the way you wanted me to. That's why. What you did was wrong." He kept trying to put the blame on me. And I refused to take that.

As long as the partners in the relationship diffuse responsibility for the violence, deny or minimize the abuse, blame the victimized person or someone's bad temper, and stay isolated from outside support, the violence will continue. Instead of separating or seeking appropriate help, they will stay together and continue the cycle of violence. In the next phase, they will attempt to recapture the myth of perfect love and avoid the painful reality that they are in a very dangerous situation.

Dating abuse doesn't start with the first punch or slap. It begins long before that with more subtle methods of gaining power and control in a relationship. Answer the following questions honestly.

1. Do you criticize your dating partner about his or her looks, clothes, or behavior?
2. Do you blame your boyfriend or girlfriend for your feelings, especially feelings of anger?
3. Do you believe that your partner can "push your buttons" and cause you to lose control and become physically aggressive?
4. Have you ever lied to your partner and gotten angry when you were caught?
5. Have you ever made derogatory sexual remarks to your partner directly, or about him or her to others?
6. Have you ever "played rough" with your partner after you were asked to stop?
7. Have you ever damaged or destroyed anything that belonged to your partner?
8. Have you ever broken any of your own possessions and blamed your boyfriend or girlfriend?
9. Does your personality or mood change radically when you drink or get high?
10. Have you ever been so drunk or high on a date that you forgot some of what went on?
11. Do you ever discourage your boyfriend or girlfriend from spending time with other friends or with family members?
12. Do you make frequent phone calls or stop by to "check up on" your partner?

13. Have you ever followed your boyfriend or girlfriend without his or her knowledge, or had friends follow for you?
14. Have you held your boyfriend or girlfriend to get them to listen to you, or to stay when he or she wanted to leave?
15. Do you expect sex as a reward for favors or kind behavior or get angry when your partner says no to you?
16. Do you ever pressure your partner to have sex or to go further than your partner wants to when making out?
17. Have you ever frightened your partner by some dangerous activity, such as driving recklessly or playing with a weapon?
18. Have you ever assaulted a boyfriend or girlfriend?
19. Have you ever threatened to harm your partner or threatened to use a weapon?
20. Have you ever threatened to kill yourself if your boyfriend or girlfriend were to leave you?
21. Have you ever threatened to kill your boyfriend or girlfriend?
22. Were you abused as a child or did you witness one of your parents abusing the other?

If you answered yes to three or more of the above questions, or have done any of these things more than once, please talk to someone right away about it. It doesn't hurt to ask about a problem, only to ignore it. Check the Sources for Help and Information at the back of the book.

 BREAKING UP, MAKING UP,

> I know sometimes he's gone too far, he's off the wall with the jealousy bit. But there was no reason for my mother to have him arrested that time. D'you know someone that doesn't fight? That doesn't have problems? Kevin means the world to me. We can work this out, for me and my baby. I want to believe him when he says he's going to change. — Cyndi

A dating couple has a strong and complex bond that may someday become the basis of a family. Changes affecting one person in the couple—a new job, flunking out of school, a car wreck—will also have a powerful impact on the other.

Because of this bond, a couple in a violent dating relationship works to survive and stay together. After an acute battering incident, both partners try to repair the damage and return to what they believe is a normal relationship. They may not agree as to who has the problem, or what normal means, but the result is the same. They cry, they apologize, they send flowers, they make promises. They do whatever it takes to heal themselves and replace the pain of abuse with the fantasy of perfect love. They do not, however, change the way they deal with stress or conflict or their roles and expectations of each other, or find outside support. So they remain at risk for future acts of violence between them, and enter the third phase of the cycle of violence.

PHASE THREE: THE HONEYMOON

To better understand the honeymoon phase, we will divide it into two parts. First there is a "remorse, repair, and reconciliation stage," when both people are coming out of the initial shock of the assault. They may be separated at this point, due to a victim's hospitalization, the abuser's arrest, or the intervention of family members or school officials who realize that it is not safe for the couple to be together.

Now begin the phone calls, the flowers, the tearful apologies, and the promises that "it will never happen again." Steve tells about the aftermath of a fight with his girlfriend:

> Leanne wouldn't answer the phone, so I went to her house. I knew I'd screwed things up for her with the band by making a scene at her gig. But I just had to get her to talk to me. I stood outside all morning, I knew she was there. I didn't know what else to do, I felt helpless without her.

Making up can be the most intimate time this couple has known. An abusive partner who is generally out of touch with his or her feelings may be overcome with remorse for the assault and looking for forgiveness. The victim is in control of what will happen next, which was not true before and during the assault. The increased intimacy and control give the false impression that the relationship is now more equal, which helps convince the abused partner to forgive and begin making up.

Leanne had this response:

> I kept thinking that it really was my fault. If I hadn't gotten one of the guys in the band to get us drinks, we probably wouldn't have had such a screaming match in front of everybody. And I know that Steve only gets jealous because he loves me. Then he shows up the next day like a whipped puppy, all teary-eyed and mushy. I tried to be cold, but when he gets that little dog look I just can't stay mad.

Because of this temporary truce in the struggle for power and control, the partners are seduced into believing that everything is perfect once again. They begin making contact and going out together and once again experience some of that wide-eyed excitement that marked the beginning of their relationship. What follows is the second part of the honeymoon phase, called the "calm, loving, respite stage," which looks like a rather normal dating relationship.

How do we know that this couple won't live happily ever after? They have made promises to each other in all sincerity that the hitting and hurting will end. They claim to love each other and appear to be happy. So, what's wrong with this picture? Everything. Everything is the same: These young people have the same unrealistic beliefs and expectations about each other; they still deal with conflicts and stress the same way; they are isolated from outside support, maybe even more so than before. The abuser has not taken responsibility for the assault; the victim is matching and accommodating; neither is able to deal with the reality of the violence or the possibility that it will happen again.

A relationship in the honeymoon phase is likely to repeat the cycle of violence all over again. Unless there are significant changes as the result of focused support and outside help, this cycle gains momentum and speed, then spins out of control until it finally, and tragically, runs aground.

HELPING AND UNDERSTANDING VICTIMS OF ABUSE

After a couple has gone through an acute battering incident and has entered the honeymoon phase, it is usually obvious to others that something is terribly wrong. The hardest thing about having a sister, friend, or teammate who is a victim of dating abuse is watching that person stay in an unsafe relationship. It is very frustrating watching people go back to a situation where they are at risk, especially if you recently helped them to get free of that control and abuse.

It is important not to judge someone who is in the throes of the honeymoon phase. When we withdraw our support because we can no longer stand to see that person suffer, we isolate the victim further. The best thing to do is to let the person know that, no matter what, you are there to offer your support. And when the person is ready to accept it, you need to be ready to provide it.

In a healthy relationship, boundaries keep people safe. Good boundaries build our confidence and give our partners clear guidelines for how we are to be treated.

For example, with parents and authority figures, we may ask, "How late can I stay out?" or "How much can I have to go to the movies?" Our parents then set the boundary by saying, "Ten-thirty," or "Eight bucks." Then we might try to negotiate, by clearly stating our needs and without making demands or getting mad. Ultimately, with a parent or other authority figure, however, we must stick to the boundaries that they set for us.

When establishing boundaries with a dating partner, however, the process is a bit different. Either partner can set limits, and both partners need to respect each other's right to do so. Here are some helpful guidelines to remember:

- You have the right to set limits, especially sexual limits, with a dating partner.

- Be assertive. You have as much right to be heard as your partner does.

- Know what you want, communicate that, and stick to it.

- You are always free to change your mind.

- Trust your feelings. If the voice in your head says, "Stop," then stop.

- Pay attention to situations that don't look or feel right, like being isolated from others or stranded in a dangerous place. If your date puts you in a risky situation, you have the right to leave as quickly as possible.

- You do not have to submit to any form of physical or verbal abuse.

It is not all right to ignore the limits you have set with a partner. Without healthy boundaries, the relationship becomes a constant struggle instead of a cooperative journey toward trust and understanding. The only rule then is that the stronger wins, the weaker loses.

It helps to understand some of the reasons why young men or women stay in abusive relationships:

- Guilt: Many victims blame themselves for the abuse, believing that it was provoked by some imperfection or failure of theirs.

- Fear: Many victims have been threatened repeatedly. They may believe they will be physically assaulted or killed, or that their partners will attempt suicide, if they try to end the relationship.

- Loneliness: Coping with an abusive partner requires a lot of energy and can take over a person's entire life. Without the relationship, the individual may feel terribly empty and alone.

- Isolation: There may be little support from family or friends to help victims overcome the obstacles that keep them in abusive relationships.

- Low self-esteem: People stay in an unhealthy relationship if they don't believe they deserve anything better. This belief is continually confirmed by the abusive behavior of the partner.

- Shame and embarrassment: It is often difficult for victims to admit to being physically or emotionally abused because they fear that others will criticize or judge them.

- Loss of status: Going out with a popular or athletic person, or even an unpopular person, has a higher social status than being single. In the world of young adults, driven by peer pressure, couple status is very hard to give up, particularly for those who believe that they are incomplete or worthless without a partner.

- Learned behavior: Women often learn to respond to abuse by being passive, dependent, submissive and quiet. Men learn the stoic, uncomplaining, "I'm tough enough to handle it" position.

No one can force another person to stop abusing a partner or to stop being a victim. All of us can, however, help in other ways. We can refuse to participate in demeaning and sexist joking. We can confront denial and blame-shifting when we encounter it. And we can be ready to provide support when someone we know is ready to break the cycle of violence and ask for help.

LOVE

What's love got to do with dating violence? Nothing. Love and abuse have nothing in common. But much emotional and physical violence happens between people who claim to love each other. We need to remove the confusion around what is and what isn't love.

Michelle has worked hard to develop her self-esteem after dating abusive partners in her early teens. She describes the different type of relationship she's in now:

> It's two people who have their own identities, their own goals, their lives; who decide they want to share with the other person; and who want to become a significant part of that other person's life. But at the same time, you're very much allowed to be who you are. That's what I like about the guy I'm dating now. I'm very much free to be who I am.

Love is supposed to make us feel good, self-confident, optimistic, and energetic. An abusive relationship makes us feel bad, insecure, depressed, and tired. Love should be playful, sensitive, and joyful. Dating violence leaves us rigid, numb, and afraid. So what makes people in the honeymoon phase think they are in love? Simple. They have never experienced what love really is.

Many of their mistaken ideas about love come from the lyrics to popular songs. At a time in our lives when we most need reliable information about members of our own and the opposite sex, there is very little. But there is radio and MTV, and young people spend lots of time listening and learning. Most song lyrics describe the pain and agony of love, but they carry other messages as well. One is that the pain is either caused by, or can be cured by, our "special someone." Another is that the greater the obstacle, the greater the love. There's the common message that all would be well if our partners would just be the way we want them to. Often songs suggest that we only have to get our partners to "make up" after a "break up," and our earlier mistakes and the damage they caused will disappear.

This is what Cyndi thinks love is all about:

> I've never doubted that Kevin loves me. That's why I can understand his jealousy, even if I don't like it. It proves he can't live without me, that he won't ever let go. I can put up with all the rest of it, because when I hear our song, *End of the Road,* I know that this is true love.

These song lyrics reinforce all the myths and mistaken beliefs we have about love. The most dangerous of these is that we should endure everything, even abuse, from a partner because "love conquers all."

There is some pain involved in dating and falling in love, but it comes from losses that are natural and part of growing. We lose our romantic illusions, our childhood innocence, the partners who don't work out. We even lose our old relationship with our families as we move out into the world on our own. But there is nothing about love that allows one person to hurt or control another. With healthy boundaries, we can enjoy the process of dating and falling in love without experiencing the type of pain caused by abusive behavior.

If you are wondering whether someone you know is being abused, ask yourself the following questions. A yes answer to any of these questions is a warning that the person you are concerned about may be in an abusive relationship.

1. Have you noticed a drop in this person's self-esteem? Is there self-criticism or self-doubt you haven't noticed before?
2. Have you noticed a change in the way the person dresses? Do his or her habits or activities suddenly seem limited?
3. Does this person have less contact than usual with family or friends, seem afraid or unable to call or visit?
4. Is this person fearful of his or her partner's jealousy and avoiding people or situations out of fear of how the partner may react?
5. Have you seen or heard this person being put down or criticized by the partner?
6. Have you witnessed physical abuse or signs of physical assault on the person—bruises, difficulty moving arms or legs, walking or breathing?

If you suspect someone you know is being abused, you cannot force that person to get help, but let him or her know that you care and that help is available. Call one of the organizations listed in Sources for Help and Information at the back of the book for advice on other ways you might help the person in this potentially dangerous situation.

When a couple enters the honeymoon following dating violence, they have not taken the time to learn from their mistakes. Nothing has changed in how they handle conflicts or their unrealistic expectations of each other. There is no outside support, and stress in the relationship has probably increased as a result of the battering incidents. Though all appears calm, this couple will start the cycle of violence again and again until they hit bottom, or until one or both of them have the courage to break the silence and reach out for help.

CHAPTER SIX

BREAKING THE SILENCE

> He kept telling me he couldn't live without me. I know now that was bull, but that's what he told me. I can remember one argument we had. He went on and on about my past and how worthless I was, and I just whipped around and said, "You know, I don't throw your past in your face, but you are always judging me and that's not fair." Our relationship was just a lot of fighting and screaming and making out, that's all it was. — Michelle

Change is not possible while abuse is going on. The cycle of violence, once it has made a complete sweep through all three phases, will continue until one or both partners reach out for help. Unbroken, the cycle intensifies in speed and force. Even the couple's separation may not be enough to keep the acts of violence from escalating, perhaps to the point of murder.

INCREASED VIOLENCE

We are all creatures of habit. We persist in our beliefs and repeat behaviors that are familiar, sometimes long after those actions or attitudes stop making sense. It's a little like getting a hand-me-down bicycle, one with difficult shiftings or hardly any brakes, that we learn to ride anyway. More than that, we develop a sense of pride because we can get around on this piece of junk. Our self-esteem is based on being able to make something work that no one else could. If we were to get a new bike, it would seem strange not to have to worry about its falling apart. We become attached to the difficulties.

Abusive relationships work just this way. The victims learn to tolerate whatever's wrong. They tell themselves they can handle it, and things are going to get better. For both partners, the relationship is familiar and more comfortable than the unknown territory of other potential relationships or the trauma of breaking up. So they stay in the cycle of violence, hope for the good times of the honeymoon, and try to survive.

Marja describes an incident that happened after she married her boyfriend, thinking that her commitment would stop him from being jealous:

> I had tried to split up, but I didn't want anyone to know, especially my folks. This was after I got fired from my job because of his harassing me at work. I was staying with a friend. I guess he followed me there. When I came out of her house, my windshield was broken. I saw him coming around the corner, and he aimed his car right at me.

Over time, the amount of emotional and physical abuse increases. Threats become shoves, shoves turn into slaps, slaps into punches. Leanne was assaulted soon after she moved in with her boyfriend:

> I had been out partying with some friends after a gig, and I came back to the apartment and passed out. I guess Steve had been looking through my journal while I was sleeping. It's where I keep lyrics I'm working on and chords and stuff. All I know is that I woke up, and he was beating me. My nose was bleeding and everything.

Also, as the cycle of violence repeats, the time lapse between assaults becomes shorter. A complete cycle may take a year or more the first time, the next time only six months, then six weeks, and so on. The periods of calm during the honeymoon nearly disappear as they are squeezed between the more frequent acute battering phases of the cycle.

With a male batterer, the emotional abuse often escalates into physical abuse during a partner's pregnancy. Once across the line between emotional and physical assault, the batterer "numbs out" and become less able to recognize his feelings. His partner becomes the enemy, and every conflict becomes a battle for power and control. Emotional abuse increases in frequency, becoming almost constant through all phases of the cycle. Physical attacks are triggered if the partner attempts to resist being controlled or to stop the emotional abuse.

Kevin described his "numbing out" when assaulting his pregnant girlfriend, Cyndi:

> Every time I get into a fight, I don't see her. I just start smashing things. And she gets in my way. I've told her not to get in my way when I go off like that.

Lisa survived an abusive dating relationship that lasted almost ten years. She wrote this poem late in that relationship.

Lisa bravely offered to share her words in the hope that someone in a similar situation won't have to feel so all alone, and will also find the courage to break the silence.

You hurt me.
I think—
He thinks I don't love him
If I just act differently
talk differently, be different . . .

I cry at night
Alone with the image
of your words
like whips
leaving blood and scars
down my back.
I think—
He doesn't know
how much I want him
I'll just hold him more
smile more, ignore more . . .

I think—
this is love
this is commitment
this is my life
I'm a strong woman
I can make it work
He loves me,
He tells me,
especially after
I cry

Often, a victim of dating abuse may try to assert herself or fight back when being assaulted. This usually escalates the abuser's use of force—increasing the chances of serious injury—and allows him to shift blame for the attack onto the victim. This can increase the victim's sense of powerlessness. Many victims develop what is called "battered woman syndrome," give up hope of surviving the abuse, and become profoundly depressed.

HITTING BOTTOM

At some point, all attempts to deny the violence fail. All the myths the victims tell themselves—or the lies they tell their friends—to keep the abuse out of sight just stop working. This experience is referred to in alcoholism recovery as "hitting bottom" and is different for each person. The one thing that people who are hitting bottom have in common is that none of them believed it could ever happen to them.

All the myths—from childhood, romantic novels and films, song lyrics—finally fall apart. The suffering endured for love's sake didn't make the relationship better or make the abuse stop. When victims realize that nothing can be done to change the behavior of an abusive dating partner, they often feel a sense of despair. But they also feel a sense of relief. They can let go of the fantasy of the "perfect partner" who can make one's life complete, and they can begin taking responsibility for their own happiness. They can begin changing the only person any of us have the power to change: oneself.

Steve, who was arrested for assault and public intoxication, recalls the morning he woke up in a jail cell:

> I couldn't believe that she would go ahead and have me arrested. I got really scared when this guy from the D.A.'s office came in and told me I was being held for assault. Nothing like this had ever happened to me before. It really forced me to put all this stuff into perspective. I mean, did I really want to go to jail?

When partners become aware of how life-threatening their violent dating relationship really is, they are forced to confront what they've lost: friends, family, status, grades, jobs, health, freedom. They can finally begin to get in touch with the hurt feelings and replace the numbness caused by the violence.

Some partners in abusive relationships attempt to escape their feelings by using drugs or alcohol. As a result, addiction and violence often overlap, and sometimes people hit bottom with both problems at the same time.

Hitting bottom marks the beginning of change. Although things may seem at their worst, they are actually starting to improve. Getting help and support to survive an abusive relationship starts when one or both of the partners can no longer deny what is going on. Both partners may feel isolated and ashamed, which makes it difficult to break down the wall they have built against the outside world. It is especially hard to tell those who may be in a position to help. Only by realizing that they cannot fix the abusive relationship alone can the victims and abusers gradually find the strength to break their silence and take the first step toward healing.

BREAKING THE SILENCE

Marja recalls the first step she took to end her isolation:

> I tried at least a dozen times to call a crisis line. I just sat there with the phone shaking in my fist. In my head were all the messages my father had drilled into me. I wasn't supposed to ask for help, that was a sign of weakness. When my mother told him about me being beaten up on our honeymoon, he had said, "She made her bed—now she can go lie in it." I realized I had cried to my mother enough times, and nothing had changed. That's when I finally made the call to a crisis line.

Breaking the silence begins the process of separating the abused partner's needs from those of the abuser. By speaking to others and making them aware of the violence that they suffered, victims develop perspective and establish a firmer hold on reality than they were able to have while in the relationship.

Whom can they tell? Often it is easier to seek help directly from those experienced at dealing with this type of situation—a school counselor or a domestic violence crisis line. Crisis-line numbers for every state and territory of the United States are listed in the Sources section of this book. The State Coalition Office can provide information about local services. Or it might be easier to tell a trusted friend, a teacher, or a doctor. The important thing is to find someone who will listen and take the problem seriously.

If you are being abused physically or in danger of other violence or know someone who is, call the police. After they have dealt with the emergency, they will refer both the victim and the assailant to the proper sources for help.

It may be necessary for you to break off all contact with a partner to prevent being hurt. The police and domestic violence services can help you to obtain emergency shelter, if necessary, or an order of protection, called a restraining order. This court order threatens an abusive partner with arrest for contacting you or following you, or for committing any further acts of emotional or physical abuse.

If you are abusing someone or are being abused, it is important that you contact services and support that deal with dating violence. The local domestic violence program, or a school counseling office, are the best places to find out about the services available in your area. Both will also be able to refer you to groups and other treatment options for young people in abusive dating situations.

Healing begins when we tell our story. But, by itself, breaking the silence will not stop the violence. If the limits set down for the protection of both partners are violated, the abuse will continue. The tendency is too strong, even with outside support, to repeat the old patterns in the relationship. It is usually necessary to end the dating relationship for the violence to end.

BREAKING UP

Ending any relationship is difficult, no matter what the circumstances. When we have outgrown a dating partner, or realize there is not enough feeling to keep the relationship going, it is very difficult to let the partner know. It's also difficult to be the one being told that it's over.

Any breakup is a loss, and the partners will feel shock, sadness, anger, relief, longing, awkwardness, and acceptance, although not necessarily in that order. Not everyone who breaks up experiences all these feelings, and the process will certainly be different for the two people involved. Breaking up is painful, but survivable. In a healthy relationship, both people can accept and respect each other's wishes. They deal with the fact that they are both changing, and that growth—even if it means growing apart—is okay.

Ending an abusive dating relationship is much more difficult. First, there is the confusion over which relationship is lost: the real one or the fantasy. The partners will need to grieve them both. They will also feel the loss of all the energy spent trying to make the relationship work, the loss of friends and family, and the loss of self-esteem.

Leanne discusses her difficult decision to break off her two-year-long relationship with Steve:

> I didn't want the relationship to be over so much as I wanted my life to be over. I thought breaking up was like death, only worse. I had never felt so sick and tired in my life. I thought there was no one who I could turn to, no one who would listen. When

> I finally made the decision that it was over, I remember saying out loud, "That's it." I immediately felt stronger, less insane. I knew it would be hard telling him and dealing with the fallout, but it seemed like there was no other way. My life seemed possible again.

Once you have decided to break up, be clear about your decision and consistent with your actions. Every contact after this decision is made gives your partner the hope that it's not really over. He or she may believe that you can patch things up, especially if you two have broken up before. Your former partner may still be in denial, and sincerely believe that it will all get better. There might also be a strong temptation for both of you to move back into the honeymoon phase, starting the cycle of violence all over again.

Remember, abusive partners believe they can control the other person. They believe they have only to apply pressure, or persuade with the right gift, to get their partners back. If being nice doesn't work, they can instantly become threatening and aggressive. People that get hurt are often trying to "deal with it" by themselves so as not to attract attention to the situation. This is a mistake. You cannot take chances with violence.

If you need to communicate with or return personal belongings to a former partner, do it through another person. If you must make contact, have a trusted friend or adult present and meet in a public place, like the principal's office or McDonald's—never alone in a car or an apartment. Manipulation, coercion, and even physical or sexual abuse do not stop just because a couple have decided to break up. Many teens, especially young women, have been abducted, raped, and even killed by their abusive partners after attempting to break off a relationship. That's why many states have passed laws against stalking to prevent an ex-partner from having an opportunity to commit an assault.

If you have any suspicion that you are at risk, ask for help. Do not try to deal with the situation alone.

LOVERS WHO BECOME KILLERS

The threat of danger from an abusive partner does not end after the couple has broken up. Often victims of dating abuse minimize the risks after the relationship ends, however, leaving police, family, and friends powerless to ensure their safety. The period following the couple's separation actually carries the greatest risk for lethal assault. A tragedy that took place in Massachusetts serves as an example of what can and does too often happen when neither partner reaches out for help.

On Sunday, February 12, 1995, twenty-eight-year-old Stephen Grunning allegedly smashed his way into the apartment of his twenty-three-year-old ex-girlfriend Rhonda Stuart less than three hours after the police had removed him from her home. There, according to a *Boston Globe* article on the following Sunday, Stephen Grunning shot Rhonda and her brother, Richard, age twenty-six, and a man that she was currently dating, Nelson DeOliviera, age twenty-three. Both men were killed. Rhonda was hospitalized.

The paper interviewed more than thirty friends and neighbors of the couple, who had much to say about their eighteen-month-long relationship. Friends described Stephen as tall and good-looking, and Rhonda as thin and pretty, with a warm smile and a huge circle of friends. They met at a club in August 1993, and began dating soon after. One of Rhonda's friends remembered that they were very happy and that problems didn't develop until months into the relationship.

It was gradual. He'd freak when she was a minute late. He'd watch every move she made at clubs. He'd call her all night long, again and again. Then I started hearing about the fist fights and emotional torment. He was so possessive. He thought he owned her.

In the summer of 1994, Stephen made a big show of kissing Rhonda during his softball games whenever he got a hit. He also made a big show of cursing her when she showed up late or spoke with another man. Once, while drinking beer after a game, he had to be restrained by teammates after throwing her against a car, friends said. Also that summer, after an argument about her driving, he began kicking her car when they stopped for gas, then kicking her, punching her, and pulling her hair. The gas station attendant called 911, but Rhonda left before police arrived. Stephen went to her apartment later that night and convinced her to make up with him.

"He seemed like such a nice guy, but he had a dark side," one of their friends said. "He was so obsessed. I always worried that it might end like this." Stephen was also described as possessive, controlling, jealous, and manipulative.

Friends reported that the couple had an up-and-down relationship. Stephen would call her vicious names and hit her when she ordered him out. He would apologize, promising never to do it again, she would take him back, and the cycle would begin anew. After Rhonda broke up with Stephen that August, he responded by taking out a restraining order against her. But a week later they were back together, and he asked the court to dismiss the order.

A week after that, Stephen was arrested when Rhonda filed a criminal complaint alleging that he beat and choked her. Later, when Rhonda tried to get the charges dismissed, authorities refused. She asked Stephen to seek counseling. According to her friends, he told her that the abuse was all her fault.

Rhonda finally broke up with Stephen for good. But a few weeks before the shootings, he was waiting for her in front of her home. She and the friend she was with drove around until they thought he was gone, but the next day she told her friend that Stephen had been hiding in the bushes. He screamed at her, asked her where she had been, and made her swear that she was not seeing a new man. She had let him into her apartment. He later got a restraining order against her, claiming that she was harassing him.

The abuse that Rhonda suffered was a poorly kept secret. Her friends said that they begged her to get a restraining order against Stephen. Her family also pleaded with her to drop him. Police said that Rhonda called just two weeks before the shootings to ask about a restraining order and was directed to Domestic Violence services for assistance. But records show she never sought an order.

At 3:30 A.M., the morning of the murders, Stephen was again waiting for Rhonda when she returned home. That night he had found out that Rhonda was dating Nelson, her friends said. Rhonda and Stephen had a loud argument, and police received reports that a man was assaulting a woman. Police responded about 4 A.M. Rhonda asked them to take Stephen away, and they sent him home in a taxi.

Two hours later, Stephen allegedly broke into Rhonda's apartment with a sledgehammer. There were screams, then shots, according to neighbors. One heard Stephen yell, "If I can't have you, no [expletive] is gonna have you!" Police said that Stephen shot and wounded Nelson, then shot him once more in the head while he lay on the floor. Richard Stuart, who had spent the last several days in his sister's apartment, was also shot to death.

CHAPTER SEVEN

CHANGING THE SYSTEM

> I knew somehow that people were beating each other all the time, other kids' parents and stuff. But you almost never heard of anyone going to jail. I always thought they made excuses around that for husbands and wives. — Linda

Dating relationships and families are both examples of social systems: networks of strong and complex ties between people. A social system works like a complex machine to keep itself running, and a change in one part of the system affects every other part. Violence in a dating relationship disrupts the balance in that system. The violence also diminishes the lives of the people in and around that system—the couple, their friends, their families.

All social systems—each with its own rules and structure—are interconnected. Just as violence affects a dating relationship or a family, violence, particularly against women, affects the larger systems of our culture and society as a whole.

The inner workings of abusive relationships apply equally to abuse of women by men, or men by women, or even to dating violence in same-sex couples. This chapter focuses on abusive and violent acts committed by men against women. In our culture, men exert power over women in many ways, and aspects of the society minimize or deny that the abusive behavior is abnormal or in any way a problem.

VIOLENCE AGAINST WOMEN

Dating and marital violence committed by men against women makes up 95 percent of all reported abuse cases. The *Journal of Emergency Nursing* reported in October 1994 that "22% to 35% of women seeking treatment at the emergency department for any complaint are there because of symptoms related to physical abuse—from suicide and depression to trauma."

A study of female high school students surveyed by *USA Today* magazine in November 1991 reports that 12 percent had experienced violent behavior by a dating partner. The students in the study felt that women's financial dependency on men and their belief that love can solve all problems both contributed to the abuse. As *Health* (July/August 1992) reported, only 16 percent of date rape is reported by teens.

Learned aggressive behavior and poor responses to stress may explain why certain men batter women. But these influences do not explain why, despite the fact that their behavior is illegal, men as a group perpetrate violence toward women.

DOUBLE STANDARD

Mack reveals some of the thinking that led to his sexual assault of a former girlfriend:

> When I'm wrestling, it's okay to go mad, get totally pumped, whatever it takes to bring my opponent to the mat. I've been trained that you go for your objective with everything you've got. But if I'm on a date, and I want to have sex, that same attitude will get me arrested. I have trouble sometimes figuring out which rules to play by.

There are many ways in which aggression is sanctioned in public life: combat in the military, arrest and imprisonment in law enforcement, competition in business and in sports. With some few exceptions, aggressive behavior by males is considered normal and desirable. By contrast, there are few legitimate uses of aggression in our private lives. But most of the violence in our culture takes place in the home. For men, the same pattern of aggression often seems to extend from their public to private lives, where it is used to maintain power and control over women.

Throughout most of secular and religious world history, women have not often held positions of authority and have been subjected to male dominance. Even today, women earn lower salaries than men earn working at the same job. There still exists a conspicuous lack of women in high-status positions in corporations and as federal officials and leaders. This biased system gives men the control of economic resources, laws, and social policies, and places very different values on the types of roles that men and women play in our culture.

The problem of violence by men against women won't stop until there is real equality of the sexes in options, careers, income, the tasks of creating a family, and attitude.

VIOLENCE IN THE MEDIA

Much of what passes for "entertainment" actually perpetuates the myths of the double standard of rights and privileges. Media has tremendous power to influence our beliefs and our emotions, regardless of the fact that the messages and manufactured images may be false.

All the comfortable stereotypes and predictable solutions we see in films and television situation comedies would have us believe that a perfect world exists that conforms to our fantasies. The carefully constructed pictures in print and film, the lyrics to popular songs, and the images on MTV encourage us to view both males and females as objects for pleasure rather than as individuals. The million or so shootings and fistfights portrayed on television encourage us to believe that violence is a way to successfully solve many of life's problems, although in reality it solves almost none. And sequel after sequel of "stalk and slash" films would have us believe that, when alone and unprotected, women are unsafe, prey to psychopaths with knives. Fear of rape and violence sets limits on the activities of women, curtailing their ability to move freely in the world, and reinforcing the myth that women are dependent upon men for protection.

Much of the process of growing up has to do with discovering that real life is not like life on television. Men feel disillusioned when they learn women don't exist solely to satisfy their needs and fulfill their fantasies, but have needs and desires of their own. Women may be surprised to learn that men, instead of being constant and protective, exploit women individually and collectively and often harm them. Both men and women experience confusion when confronted with the living, breathing, very real human they originally thought was their "special someone."

By being aware of how the media reflects and reinforces destructive stereotypes, especially the helplessness and inequality of women, we can loosen its destructive hold on our beliefs and behavior.

HOPE FOR THE FUTURE

Acts of abuse are motivated by issues of power and control. Any relationship based on a struggle for control can have only one winner and one loser. For both partners to win, the system must change into a cooperative one.

To make that change, on a personal level, we can refuse to be abused, refuse to abuse, and refuse to condone the abuse of others. We can also refuse to succumb to the sexual stereotypes that form the basis for ideas and behaviors that support sexual and human inequality.

You can participate in creating a world without violence. The first step is to make sure your dating relationship is based on reality, equality, and mutual respect.

The questions below were asked of a group of college students in a study conducted by Gloria Fischer at Washington State University. Take the survey yourself. Simply check whether you agree or disagree with each statement.

Is it all right if a male holds a female down and forces her to engage in intercourse if:

	YES	NO
1. He spent a lot of money on her?	____	____
2. He is so turned on he thinks he can't stop?	____	____
3. She has had sexual intercourse with other guys?	____	____
4. She is stoned or drunk?	____	____
5. She says she will have sex with him, but changes her mind?	____	____
6. She lets him touch her above the waist?	____	____
7. They have dated a long time?	____	____
8. She has had sex with him before?	____	____
9. She led him on?	____	____
10. She is wearing suggestive clothing?	____	____
11. She is hitchhiking?	____	____
12. She is out by herself late at night?	____	____
13. She is living with him, but they are not married?	____	____
14. She is married to him?	____	____
15. She is married to him, but they are currently separated?	____	____

A majority of the students who participated in this study answered yes to at least one question. In any one of these situations, the man's behavior constitutes a criminal offense—rape. Regardless of the justification, the woman was not consenting and the man used force. Why do you think those students believe it is all right to force someone to have sex?

If you also answered yes to any of the above, ask for help from an adult or teacher you trust. You need to learn about safe boundaries before you engage in sexual behavior. There are no circumstances that make it all right to have sex with someone without that person's consent. Don't end up in a situation where your rights are being violated, or where you are violating the rights of others.

GLOSSARY

abuse: using words or actions to mistreat, harm, or change someone's mind. See also *assault* and *violence.*

accommodation: the inability or unwillingness to express reservation or disappointment with a partner's attitude or behavior.

addiction: a dependent relationship upon some mood-altering chemical or behavior, often with life-threatening consequences.

aggression: the attempt to control someone else's actions by physical or emotional means. See also *assertion.*

assault: any attempt to hurt someone, either physically or verbally. Physical assault includes any use or threat of use of a weapon, hitting, slapping, pushing, holding persons against their will, unwanted sexual advances, or subjecting someone to dangerous or reckless behavior. Verbal assault includes screaming, cursing, threats, put-downs, name-calling, or belittling.

assertion: the attempt to set a boundary by telling someone what one wants or is willing, or unwilling, to do. Unlike acts of aggression, assertive behavior does not violate the rights of others.

blame-shifting: transferring responsibility for an assault from the batterer to the victim by focusing on their actions.

consent: explicit approval given to a partner for a shared intimacy or activity, without coercion or fear of punishment.

cycle of violence: a recurring pattern common to abusive dating relationships consisting of a tension building phase, an acute battering phase, and a honeymoon phase.

date rape: forced sexual intercourse or other sexual activity between two persons who are dating to which one person has not given consent.

dating: any or all of the ways that two people attempt to start or further an intimate relationship. For example, going out on "dates," spending time together as a couple alone or with others, regular conversations by phone, and engaging in physical contact ranging from handholding to more intimate sexual activity.

denial: the refusal to believe that acts of violence or abuse took place, or that they were meant to be harmful.

equality: a relationship in which both or all parties have the same options and equal power.

love: a strong and deep respect and regard for the welfare of another person, as well as the desire to be with and receive the affection and respect of that person.

matching: the attempt to shape attitudes or behaviors to fulfill the expectations of a dating partner.

minimization: attempts to lessen the seriousness and importance of an abusive behavior or incident.

self-esteem: appreciation of one's own value, individuality, and rights, particularly in relationships with others.

stereotyping: defining oneself or others by only certain traits and features, often grossly exaggerated, and ignoring unique qualities and personal feelings and characteristics.

violence: any attempt to force persons to do or to stop doing something against their will through emotional or physical means.

SOURCES FOR HELP AND INFORMATION

This is a list of phone numbers and addresses for national and state crisis centers and hotlines that provide help for participants in violent and abusive relationships.

Call the numbers in your state listing for shelters and treatment programs in your area. Also check the Self Help Guide in the front of any NYNEX phone directory for violence prevention services in your area. They are usually listed under the heading "Battered Women."

NATIONAL RESOURCES

AIDS HOTLINE
1-800-342-2437

AL-ANON FAMILY
GROUP
WORLD SERVICES
P.O. Box 862, Midtown Station
New York, NY 10018-0862
Phone: 212-302-7240

ALCOHOL AND DRUG
COUNSELING HOTLINE
1-800-ALCOHOL

ALCOHOLICS
ANONYMOUS WORLD
SERVICES
P.O. Box 459
Grand Central Station
New York, NY 10163
Phone: 212-686-1100

CHILD FIND, INC
P.O. Box 277
New Paltz, NY 12561
Phone: 1-800-I AM LOST

FAMILY VIOLENCE PROJECT
Building One, Suite 200
1001 Potrero Avenue
San Francisco, CA 94110
Phone: 415-821-4553

INCEST SURVIVORS
ANONYMOUS
P.O. Box 5613
Long Beach, CA 90805-0613

NATIONAL CENTER FOR
MISSING AND
EXPLOITED CHILDREN
2102 Wilson Boulevard
Suite 550
Arlington, VA 22201
Phone: 1-800-THE LOST

NATIONAL COALITION
AGAINST DOMESTIC
VIOLENCE
P.O. Box 18749
Denver, CO 80218-0749
Phone: 303-839-1852

NATIONAL COCAINE
HOTLINE
1-800-COCAINE

NATIONAL ORGANIZATION
FOR MEN AGAINST SEXISM
(NOMAS)
Ashtabula, OH 44004
Phone: 412-731-2234

STATE RESOURCES

Alabama Coalition Against
Domestic Violence
P.O. Box 4762
Montgomery, AL 36101
Phone: 205-832-4842

Alaska Network on Domestic
Violence and Sexual Assault
130 Seward Street
Room 501
Juneau, AK 99801
Phone: 907-586-3650

Arizona Coalition Against
Domestic Violence
100 West Camelback Road
Suite 109
Phoenix, AZ 85013
Phone: 602-273-5900
1-800-782-6400

Arkansas Coalition Against
Violence to Women and
Children
7509 Cantrell Road, Suite 213
Little Rock, AR 72207
Phone: 501-663-4668
1-800-332-4443

California Alliance Against
Domestic Violence
619 13th Street, Suite 1
Modesto, CA 95354
Phone: 415-457-2464

Colorado Domestic Violence
Coalition
P.O. Box 18902
Denver, CO 80218
Phone: 303-573-9018

Connecticut Coalition Against
Domestic Violence
135 Broad Street
Hartford, CT 06105
Phone: 203-524-5890
1-800-281-1481

Delaware Battered Women's
Hotline
c/o Child, Inc.
507 Philadelphia Pike
Wilmington, DE 19809
Phone: 302-762-6110

D.C. Coalition Against
Domestic Violence
P.O. Box 76069
Washington, DC 20013
Phone: 202-783-5332

Florida Coalition Against
Domestic Violence
1521 Killearn Center Blvd.
Tallahassee, FL 32308
Phone: 904-668-6862
         1-800-500-1119

Georgia Advocates for
Battered Women and
Children
250 Georgia Avenue SE
   Suite 308
Atlanta, GA 30312
Phone: 404-524-3847
         1-800-643-1212

Hawaii State Committee on
Family Violence
2500 Pali Highway
Honolulu, HI 96817
Phone: 808-595-3900

Idaho Coalition Against
Sexual and Domestic
Violence
200 North Fourth Street
   Suite 10
Boise, ID 83702
Phone: 203-384-0419

Illinois Coalition Against
Domestic Violence
937 South Fourth Street
Springfield, IL 62703
Phone: 217-789-2830

Indiana Coalition Against
Domestic Violence
2511 East 46th Street
Indianapolis, IN 46202
Phone: 317-641-1912
         1-800-332-7385

Iowa Coalition Against
Domestic Violence
1540 High Street, Suite 100
Des Moines, IA 50309
Phone: 515-244-8028

Kansas Coalition Against
Sexual and Domestic
Violence
820 SE Quincy, Suite 416-B
Topeka, KS 66612
Phone: 913-232-9784

Kentucky Domestic Violence
Association
P.O. Box 356
Frankfort, KY 40602
Phone: 502-875-4132

Louisiana Coalition Against
Domestic Violence
P.O. Box 3053
Hammond, LA 70404-3053
Phone: 504-542-4446

Maine Coalition for Family
Crisis Services
359 Main Street
Bangor, ME 04402
Phone: 207-941-1194

Maryland Network Against
Domestic Violence
11501 Georgia Avenue
Suite 403
Silver Spring, MD 20902-1955
Phone: 301-942-0900

Massachusetts Coalition of
Battered Women Service
Groups
210 Commercial Street
3rd Floor
Boston, MA 02109
Phone: 617-248-0922

Michigan Coalition Against
Domestic Violence
P.O. Box 16009
Lansing, MI 48901
Phone: 517-484-2924

Minnesota Coalition for
Battered Women
1619 Dayton Avenue
Suite 303
St. Paul, MN 55104
Phone: 612-646-0994

Mississippi Coalition Against
Domestic Violence
5455 Executive Place
Jackson, MS 39206
Phone: 601-981-9196

Missouri Coalition Against
Domestic Violence
331 Madison Street
Jefferson City, MO 65101
Phone: 314-634-4161

Montana Coalition Against
Domestic Violence
1236 North 28th Street
Suite 103
Billings, MT 59101
Phone: 406-245-7990

Nebraska Domestic Violence
and Sexual Assault Coalition
315 South 9th, Suite 18
Lincoln, NE 68508
Phone: 402-476-6256

Nevada Network Against
Domestic Violence
2100 Capurro Way, Suite E
Sparks, NV 89431
Phone: 702-358-1171
    1-800-500-1556

New Hampshire Coalition
Against Domestic & Sexual
Violence
P.O. Box 353
Concord, NH 03302-0353
Phone: 603-224-8893
    1-800-852-3388

New Jersey Coalition for
Battered Women
2620 Whitehorse/Hamilton
    Square Road
Trenton, NJ 08690
Phone: 609-584-8107
    1-800-572-7233

New Mexico State Coalition
Against Domestic Violence
P.O. Box 25363
Albuquerque, NM 87125
Phone: 505-246-9240
    1-800-773-3645

New York State Coalition
Against Domestic Violence
79 Central Avenue
Albany, NY 12206
Phone: 518-432-4864
1-800-942-6906 (English)
1-800-942-6908 (Spanish)

North Carolina Coalition
Against Domestic Violence
P.O. Box 27701
Durham, NC 27717
Phone: 919-956-9124

North Dakota Council on
Abused Women's Services
418 East Rosser Avenue
Suite 320
Bismarck, ND 58501
Phone: 701-255-6240
1-800-472-2911

Ohio Domestic Violence
Network
4041 North High Street
Suite 101
Columbus, OH 43214
Phone: 614-784-0023
1-800-934-9840

Oklahoma Coalition on
Domestic Violence and
Sexual Assault
2200 Classen Boulevard
Suite 610
Oklahoma City, OK 73106
Phone: 405-557-1210
1-800-522-9054

Oregon Coalition Against
Domestic and Sexual
Violence
520 N.W. Davis Street
Suite 310
Portland, OR 97209
Phone: 503-239-4486
1-800-622-3782

Pennsylvania Coalition
Against Domestic Violence
6400 Flank Drive, Suite 1300
Harrisburg, PA 17112
Phone: 717-545-6400
1-800-932-4632

Rhode Island Coalition
Against Domestic Violence
324 Broad Street
Central Falls, RI 02863
Phone: 401-723-3051
1-800-494-8100

South Carolina Coalition
Against Domestic Violence
and Sexual Assault
P.O. Box 7776
Columbia, SC 29202-7776
Phone: 803-254-3699

South Dakota Coalition
Against Domestic Violence
and Sexual Assault
3220 South Highway 281
Aberdeen, SD 57401
Phone: 605-225-5122

Tennessee Task Force Against
Domestic Violence
P.O. Box 120972
Nashville, TN 37212-0972
Phone: 615-386-9406

Texas Council on Family
Violence
8701 North Mopac
  Expressway, Suite 450
Austin, TX 78759
Phone: 512-794-1133

Utah Domestic Violence
Advisory Council
120 North 200 West
Salt Lake City, UT 84145
Phone: 801-538-4078

Vermont Network Against
Domestic Violence
and Sexual Assault
P.O. Box 405
Montpelier, VT 05601
Phone: 802-223-1302

Virginians Against Domestic
Violence
2850 Sandy Bay Road
  Suite 101
Williamsburg, VA 23185
Phone: 804-221-0990
  1-800-838-8238

Washington State Coalition
Against Domestic Violence
200 W Street, SE, Suite B
Turnwater, WA 98501
Phone: 206-352-4029
  1-800-562-6025

West Virginia Coalition
Against Domestic Violence
P.O. Box 85
181B Main Street
Sutton, WV 26601-0085
Phone: 304-765-2250
  1-800-352-6513

Wisconsin Coalition Against
Domestic Violence
1400 East Washington
  Suite 103
Madison, WI 53703
Phone: 608-255-0539

Wyoming Coalition Against
Domestic Violence & Sexual
Assault
341 East E Street, Suite 135A
Casper, WY 82601
Phone: 307-266-4334
  1-800-990-3877

PUERTO RICO

Comision para los Asuntos de
la Mujer
Calle San Francisco 151-153
Viejo San Juan
San Juan, PR 00901
Phone: 809-722-2907

VIRGIN ISLANDS

Women's Coalition of St.
Croix
P.O. Box 2734
Christiansted, St. Croix
U.S.V.I. 00802
Phone: 809-773-9272

Women's Resource Center
8 Kongens Gade
St. Thomas, U.S.V.I. 00802
Phone: 809-776-3966

INDEX

Honeymoon period, 44, 59, 69-71, 75, 78

Information resources, 103-108
Initial attraction, 24
Intimacy, 28, 41, 55, 60
Isolation, 36, 45, 61-62, 65, 74

Jealousy, 42, 46-49
Journal of Emergency Nursing, 94
Justice Department statistics, 18

Koop, C. Everett, 18

Learned behavior, 74
Limit setting, 72-73
Loneliness, 73
Love, myths and mistaken beliefs about, 75-76

Macho role, 38
Makeup period, 44, 59, 69-71, 75, 78
Male/female roles, 18-19, 29, 38-39
Manipulation, 43
Matching, 32-34, 71
Media images, 27, 96-97
Minimization, 60, 65
Mixed messages, 26-28
Movie stars, 23
Myths about dating violence, 19, 30

National Crime Survey, 18
National resources, 103-104

Parents, abuse of, 29
Peer pressure, 74
Pets, 54, 58

Physical abuse, 54
Police, 86
Possessiveness, 42, 46-49
Power, struggle for, 42-43, 66-67
Pregnancy, abuse during, 81
Property damage, 54, 58

Rape, 98-99
Recording artists, 23
Remorse, repair, and reconciliation stage of honeymoon period, 69-70
Rules, in relationships, 31-32

Same-sex relationships, 39, 93
School pressures, 45
Self-defense, 60-61
Self-esteem, 19, 26-28, 30, 45, 55, 74, 80
Setting limits, 72-73
Sex object, 39
Sexual abuse, 54, 55
Sexual harassment, 39-40
Shame and embarrassment, 74
Social pressures, 36-37
Social systems, 93
Song lyrics, 75-76
"Special someone" fantasy, 23-26, 28, 34, 41, 76
State Coalition Office, 85-86
State resources, 104-108
Status, loss of, 74
Stereotyping, 36-40, 96, 97
"Storybook" relationship, 35
Stress, 45
Stuart, Rhonda, 89-92
Stuart, Richard, 89, 92

Tension-building phase, 44-52, 58
Trust, 19, 28, 45, 52, 55, 60

ABOUT THE AUTHOR

John Hicks is the former director of Men Choosing to Change, a treatment program in Bartlesville, Oklahoma. He was also staff psychotherapist and child advocate for the Oklahoma shelter Women & Children in Crisis.

Mr. Hicks has lectured nationally on the subjects of spouse abuse and dating abuse, conducted seminars and groups on dating violence in schools, and trained staff for both shelter and school-based programs. He facilitates groups on dating violence at schools in New Hampshire and Massachusetts.

John Hicks is also the author of *Drug Addiction: No Way I'm an Addict,* soon to be published by The Millbrook Press.